THE RIGHT PEOPLE IN THE RIGHT JOBS

The Right People In The Right Jobs

Second edition

John Finnigan

Gower

First published 1973 by Business Books Limited

Second edition published by
Gower Publishing Company Limited
Aldershot, Hants, England

British Library Cataloguing in Publication Data

Finnigan, John
   The right people in the right jobs.—2nd ed.
   1. Personnel management
   I. Title
   658.3   HF5549

ISBN 0-566-02360-1

Typeset by Guildford Graphics Limited, Guildford, Surrey

Printed and bound in Great Britain by
Biddles Ltd, Guildford and King's Lynn

Contents

Preface

The first edition of this book, written in 1973, contained
warnings about overmanning by indiscriminate addition of
people in the absence of adequate job definitions, about
amateurish methods of matching people to working situations and about the importance of utilising the abilities of
the working team to the full. Since then worldwide recession
has highlighted the human consequences of the woefully
inadequate productivity of the late 1970s and early 1980s.

Whilst this second edition is written against a very
different background the messages it has to deliver are
remarkably similar. They are not, however, concerned with
warnings but with the actions required in the aftermath of
recession when the need to strengthen businesses after
severe cutting down makes it essential to get the right people
in the right jobs. Developing countries have a similar need
but for a different reason. They face the problem of replacing
expatriates by nationals and transferring the necessary
technical and managerial skills in the process.

This second edition is, therefore, more international in its
approach and whilst it is inevitably United Kingdom based
the stages and methods still apply in countries as far apart as
Hong Kong and Nigeria. Growth and survival of managers

in any country will depend upon their ability to build the right team and to motivate and develop it so that there is the maximum amount of participation and utilisation of all talents and abilities.

There should be no misunderstanding about the intended readership of this book. It is not designed for professional personnel people who will (or should) be familiar with its contents. It is written for busy line managers who wish to cover this ground without delving into the lengthy, and often theoretical, literature of personnel management. If it helps them to be the right people in the right jobs themselves it will have served a useful purpose. Insofar as it is intended to be topical it is accepted that the delay between writing and publishing will reduce its topicality. In matters such as United Kingdom legislation the book sets the scene, goes into principles and points the line manager in the direction of keeping up to date. The book serves, therefore, as a kind of foundation upon which to keep on building the future.

John Finnigan

1 The Underutilised Resource: People

Management is the using of resources to achieve results. These resources are of two sorts. First there is the supply of people, money, machines and material and second there is the supply of ideas, leadership, inspiration and confidence, without which results are not possible. It would be reasonable to suppose that the first sort of supply is not so easy to come by as the second, but, in fact, contemporary management is currently under criticism for its inadequate supply of ideas and declining calibre in the period of abundance in money and people that now seems to be over. This lack on the part of management has been seen as a major contribution to the current national frustration and waste of talent. (Those responsible have often fallen victim to the results of their own inadequacy.) The temptation to add people and things to businesses instead of organisation and control has led inexorably to the current situation where resources are out of balance. The day of reckoning had to come.

BUDGETING FOR RESOURCES

The management ritual of budgeting, which includes the allocation of money to be spent on people and things, is well

1

established. This ritual comforts many who practise it. They believe that management is taking place because they are using the disciplines of resource examination and forward planning. When managers are either unable or unwilling to work out the future needs of their departments they produce guesses based on the 'same as last year with a bit added on for contingencies and inflation' approach. When the results of the budgeting ritual are related to individual cost centres, the process is known as budgetary control. In departments using machinery the additional ritual of writing down, writing off or allowing for maintenance charges is part of this control and it exercises the ingenuity of both the user and the accountant.

The advent of objectives or target setting generated high hopes that these rituals could be related to something more tangible, but the results have been disappointing. Although these principles are generally understood and applauded, they have rarely been applied in any rigorous way. Corporate planning has suffered a similar fate and attempts to introduce a scientific approach to provision of future resources have, regrettably, made only limited progress, often because of an absence of management accountancy. Against this background it is difficult to provoke interest in, and attention to, budgeting and planning for people. Nevertheless, the survival of management itself depends upon it and corporate planning is a nonsense without it. It is, unfortunately, surrounded in mystery, absent from the serious and sustained researches of the behavioural sciences, excluded from financial considerations and accountancy auditing. In fact it seems to be just too difficult – but is it?

THE VALUE OF PEOPLE

Assigning a value to people is a new concept. Managers know about the costs associated with people – the costs of recruiting, training and development by way of courses – and a knowledge of these costs is accepted as a management responsibility. Budgets will normally include allowances for these matters in addition to salary, pension, fringe benefits and other financial commitments attached to people when they are added to the payroll. Training and development costs can be included without much difficulty, and will include such factors as course fees, materials, premises, salaries and expenses while in training situations, either in-company or externally.

To ask 'What is the value of training and what is the return upon the money invested in it?' produces a surprisingly blank response. Various approaches to evaluation of training have been devised by both individuals and organisations, such as the United Kingdom training boards, but they grind to a halt when a specific answer is required. The development of people by training activities set in relation to return upon investment, and not as an act of faith, is in itself a doubtful concept. It might be reasonable to suggest that without an answer to the return upon investment question there can be no case for training as a development of the value of people, and that the only justifiable activity would be training for the job by way of instruction in techniques and routines. Management training concerned with intangibles such as leadership, creativity and getting the best out of resources, especially people, has no hope at the moment if it is to be justified as a useful return upon the investment in it.

This will suffice to illustrate to the line manager the concept of value as opposed to cost. If management responsibility is to ensure immediate and long-term profitability by present-day investment in resources to produce capital assets capable of generating an acceptable return, the line manager cannot allow his attention to be restricted to things. It must include people and it must take account of their present value as future profit generators, their rate of deterioration or vocational obsolescence and the investment needed to maintain or increase their value with the passage of time.

The absence of a system or approach for doing this is recognised as a serious block. The argument that it costs too much in time and money to create such a system is a powerful one, and the pressure of other short-term high-priority matters will push the idea into the background. This outlook in relation to people has contributed considerably to the depression in status and authority of the personnel function. This depression has had now well-known disastrous effects upon the lives and the morale of many people and contributed to the decline and extinction of many employers. The wastage and underutilisation of human talent cannot any longer be tolerated and the adoption by management of the concept of people having value rather than cost will mark a new starting point in their concern for this wastage. Ethical and moral objections to regarding people as a commodity will have to be combated by the new managers who follow a value, or return upon investment approach. The suspicion that such managers will be unsympathetic to the application of human relations considerations in their departments, and that they will be motivated by a strictly mercenary outlook, will have to be dissipated.

RELATIONSHIPS

Organisational theories have attempted to clarify the roles of managers involved in line management or in supporting roles. Line managers cannot, and usually would not, seek to deprive themselves of the help of specialists outside their own departments but occupying a similar place in the firm's hierarchy, or indeed outside the company. They need help in complex matters of finance, marketing, computer applications, planning and control, and similarly in matters of personnel and training. Although roles and relationships may be perfectly clear on the organisation chart, the establishment of working relationships depends upon the managers concerned and the extent to which they will seek, and accept, help and guidance, while retaining their departmental autonomy. The relationship will be influenced by the prevailing wavelength of their communications. Conflicting priorities and objectives will not help and, especially in employee matters, line managers will, it is to be hoped, rightly claim that they know their people better than a specialist outside the department.

The line manager's relationship with the personnel specialist is such that discussion between them about adding people to the payroll can be tricky. When there are departmental resignations line managers often insist that they need exact replacements and ask the personnel manager to find them. The sort of personnel manager who is concerned about the size of the total company payroll and the effective utilisation of everybody on it will wonder whether this replacement is necessary and, if so, should it be an exact repeat. It must, however, be acknowledged that many personnel managers do not think along these lines. They do recruit an identical replacement in order to avoid managerial conflict.

Management principles state that the line manager must be responsible for the staffing of his department and that the personnel manager must be concerned with the total staffing situation and not allow managers to waste the company's human resources and, consequently, its money. The success of this delicate relationship, so open to the play of conflicting personalities and interests, is entirely dependent upon the managers concerned. The relationship has to be cultivated, it cannot be produced to order. The question 'What is the value to this company of each individual employee either as an individual or member of a team?' should be asked continually by both managers. It should be asked when people are recruited and when their performance, progress and survival are being appraised.

Immediately an interest in the value of people is taken, the problems of communication and relationships, which includes those of different points of view, pressures and priorities, will be there. Admittedly, the line manager cannot often have the same point of view as the personnel specialist, but the factors which make up his view will have to be the subject of more line management appreciation if the human asset is to be made to count. Some line managers will need to be educated to this appreciation; it may have to be imposed on some by the directors; and for others who are already incorporating it into their style of management it will appear obvious.

ROLE OF THE COMPANY PERSONNEL FUNCTION

One of the least respected and underappreciated functions in industry and business organisations has been, and regrettably in many cases still is, the personnel function. The training aspect of it received a considerable boost and increase in status as a result of the Industrial Training Act 1964, which attached considerable sums of money to it. The industrial relations aspect has received a similar boost as a result of legislation which has attached order, responsibility and a legal framework to it. The general aspects of personnel management have benefited by specific legislation but in the last analysis matters associated with getting the right person in the right job can expect to gain stature and respect only if they contribute to the company's development and profitability. It cannot be done by legislation. The current depressed status of the personnel function has been caused by several factors which are understood by personnel professionals and this understanding can be turned to advantage in developing the personnel function and the line manager's part in it. These factors are:

(a) Full employment after the war, leading to indiscriminate addition of people to the payroll against inadequate or non-existent job descriptions, people more capable of coping with volume of work than quality or efficiency.
(b) A general obsession with the present and an inability to develop thoughts and plans for the future.
(c) The lack of a recognised training programme and professional examination qualification for personnel staff, and the introduction of inappropriate types of people among them.
(d) Confusion about the place of personnel management in the organisational structure. Grey areas exist which lead to difficult relationships between personnel staff and line managers.
(e) Disproportionate emphasis upon social and welfare aspects diverting attention from personnel management in its up-to-date form.

The situation is, however, changing and there is evidence that the personnel function has gained in status because of the high cost of getting and retaining people, the introduction and growing acceptance of techniques like management by objectives, job evaluation, motivation and job enrichment.

The introduction of personnel management subjects into university and college courses is bringing a new generation of graduates in arts, sociology, behavioural science and industrial management into personnel jobs. The United Kingdom's Institute of Personnel Management's new requirement that membership should be dependent upon taking a course of instruction and passing the appropriate examinations, as distinct from qualifying after a period of time in the job, is having a welcome elevating effect.

Against this background it is now useful to look at the key functions of personnel management. They can be summarised as follows:

1 To ensure an adequate supply of the right people, at the right time, to do jobs adequately defined.
2 To ensure that the most effective use and development of human resources is made.
3 To ensure that methods of assessing performance, motivating and rewarding people are adequate and equitable.
4 To ensure that the company's environment, facilities and amenities are appropriate for the achievement of success in these key tasks.
5 To ensure that the company operates within the law so far as its employment of people is concerned by implementing statutory requirements and recommendations of organisations with which the company is concerned as employers.
6 To participate in matters of industrial relations as defined by national and local agreements and also in procedures required by law.

These responsibilities cannot be totally delegated to the personnel function. They must form the basis of company policy, defined by its board of directors, and require the involvement of managers and supervisors at all levels. A cooperative relationship between the personnel function and other company functions must develop attitudes appropriate to these tasks for the benefit of the whole company.

In companies with a full-time personnel manager with an appropriate staff, there need be no reason why a competent specialist should have difficulty in managing these key areas effectively. It is in smaller firms, where full-time specialist appointments cannot be justified but where attention to the key functions is equally important, possibly more so, that difficulties can arise. But whether these matters receive attention from a personnel manager, line manager or an outside consultant, there is no doubt that any firm who wishes to make progress in the 1980s must give them attention.

As this book is written primarily for line managers; the implication is that there will not usually be access to a personnel manager. It is, however, likely that line managers who do have this access will find much in this book relevant to their dealings with specialists. The employee responsibility may be full-time, part-time or externally assigned to a consultant, but whatever the case it must be a clearly identified and understood responsibility supported by authority and accountability.

MANAGEMENT PROBLEMS FOR THE PERSONNEL MANAGER

If getting the right person for the right job depends upon higher calibre personnel management, personnel managers of the future will have to overcome entrenched resistance to the innovations they may have in mind that will contribute significantly to this raising of status and calibre. As the specialists responsible for total company manpower, operating within the key areas, they will have to sell new thinking to the line managers. They will be co-ordinating approaches to training, manpower development and performance appraisal schemes, which are difficult enough in themselves, to individual managers and their departments. Their human relationships will be severely tested in attempts to get already busy line managers involved in the key personnel areas.

One of the major causes of slow progress in these matters has been the lack of incentive for the line departments to give them adequate priority. Exhortation and persuasion have had limited success and the return on investment has been unidentified. The new thinking, directed to placing value instead of cost on better personnel management, will provide management with the incentive to take it more seriously. Success will be related to the following:

(a) The placing of the personnel management function at the heart of the business, not on its fringes, with sufficient status and authority to command attention.

(b) Access to the firm's policy makers who, while not always able to produce exact information, will be able to produce sufficient informed opinion to act as a foundation for the operation of manpower planning, corporate planning, management by objectives and productivity plans as serious activities.

(c) Availability of information which does not exist for any other purpose, but which is probably badly needed for other purposes, and which those concerned will maintain is too difficult and expensive to find.

(d) Accountants who are prepared to modify some of their own rituals and introduce management accountancy, as opposed to historical bookkeeping, as a live information and forward planning service for not only the personnel manager but all line managers.

(e) Access to the computer for providing and storing information about people and their attributes.

(f) Ability to identify minimum information needs and be specific about the reasons for needing it. This will not be confined to the financial information previously mentioned but will embrace production control, marketing and selling, design and research.

(g) Access to outside specialists such as management consultants, universities and research organisations operating in areas such as sociology, behavioural science and occupational psychology.

(h) Acceptance of the concept of value of people and a personal dedication to tackling the investigation and development of it.

(i) Time to spend on the key areas, time to think and the opportunity to experiment in down-to-earth ways.

PERSONNEL MANAGEMENT PROBLEMS OF THE LINE MANAGER

To the manager of a business profit centre the first priority is profit, and interest in return on investment in manpower will be the same as interest in return on any other resources. Requirements of line managers will include the following:

(a) A personnel manager within a company must understand the line manager's pressures and take account of them in any personnel and training activities advocated.
(b) Statements of company objectives with as much information as possible about corporate plans so that the department's objectives, especially those related to the people, can be worked out.
(c) The opportunity to organise the work of the department so that it is receptive to job enrichment, performance appraisal, training and development.
(d) Access to a company manpower development and utilisation plan allowing for the planned movement of people to acquire special knowledge or experience.
(e) Assessment of departmental performance by availability of cost, value and profit centres which will expose strong and weak areas on the basis of fact.
(f) Terms of reference which require assessment of the value of people as part of the annual budgeting procedure.
(g) Stimulation by the total environment being receptive to ideas, discussion with line colleagues plus encouragement to take interest in outside activities such as relevant seminars.

VALUE CONCEPT IN RELATION TO PEOPLE

The concept of value as distinct from cost has already been introduced, but anyone developing an interest in it will be handicapped by lack of experience, absence of precedents and the elementary state of the thinking about it. As a new aspect of personnel management it is ideal for attention by forward-looking personnel people. The precise definition of value in this context is by no means obvious. In fact the state of knowledge about industrial and business value is still very dependent upon personal interpretation or opinion, given the current general state of job insecurity and inflation. Despite this lack it is, however, possible to examine some value definitions in relation to people.

BASIC VALUE

This is equal to the basic cost of an individual to the employer. This includes not only direct matters such as salary, pension and insurance, etc. but the cost of the space occupied by the furniture used, expendables, such as paper and telephone calls, and costs of any personal staff such as a secretary. Clearly it would be impossible and unnecessary to apply this exercise to every individual and as a short cut categorisation followed by the application of a multiplying factor to, for example, the salary of people in the category would be sufficiently accurate for looking at value by this means.

This approach is still predominantly one of cost rather than value, but in the absence of other means of measuring value this exercise is worth doing as a starting point in allocating priorities for work demands from the more expensive sections of a department. If the output of the section can be measured or graded, the application of a basic value concept can give a crude, but better than nothing, indication of productivity (productivity being defined as output per person per unit of time). Although a long way from measurement of value as a concept in management, this simple exercise will reveal much. The amount of investment in what the manager may regard as low-priority or marginal departmental activities may be surprisingly high when it is compared with similar information about the more obvious high-priority activities related to the reason for the very existence of the department.

REPLACEMENT VALUE

A concept noted by Professor Rensis Likert, Director of the Institute of Social Research, University of Michigan. He is reported as asking the question:

Suppose your chief executive went to work this morning and found all the people had left. Buildings, machinery and financial resources remained; all the jobs were there to be done, but there was nobody to do them. How much would it cost to engage the people to fill the vacancies, train them to do the work as well as it is done now and make it into an organisation as effective as the present one?

This illustrates what is meant by replacement value.

MARKET VALUE

This is what an employee will get if tested on the open market by applying for other jobs. This is often of more value to the individual than the employer and it is not unusual for ambitious individuals to test themselves by applying for other appointments as a means of measuring their position in financial terms. The reverse of this from the employer's point of view is to reflect upon the salary which would have to be paid to a new employee if the present one leaves.

MAINTENANCE VALUE

An approach which is related to the passing of time. Though a piece of Georgian silver will increase in value, a person will probably not. During the early stages of a career, when training, experience and knowledge are being injected, clearly value is increasing. Deterioration begins after settlement into a steady appointment. The addition of routines and steady procedures to a job identify the need for maintenance if levels of performance are to be sustained.

In fast-moving and highly technical businesses the likelihood of being left behind is a real one. Like that of machinery, people's value depreciates and with the passage of time the return on investment will drop unless there is a further injection of value. The concern behind maintenance value is for the continuing acceptable level of performance. Improvement in performance must be approached by motivational activities or job enrichment by means of value addition.

TRANSFER VALUE

A concept unknown outside professional football but readily understood in that type of business where the law of supply and demand is prevalent and the appreciation that a top-class article will demand a top-class price is not in need of any explanation. There is no confusion, for example, about initial and investment value of professional football players.

It is interesting to speculate on how long it will be before firms will be prepared to bid for a top-class design engineer and negotiate with companies in addition to the individual. This revolutionary approach to value has been commented upon by James S. Hekimian and Curtis H. Jones in the *Harvard Business Review* using the basis that assets can only have real value when there is an alternative use for them which enables them to define opportunity value. In a bidding situation the bidder is thinking of the increased profit which can be earned by attracting a scarce or specially qualified person and the transfer, or opportunity, fee can be calculated accordingly. Such a system may apply just as sensibly to firms as to football clubs, especially where a firm is hanging on to a person who is, frankly, too good for it and where full potential cannot be realised. The national problem of fully utilising native talent is aggravated by such situations and the opportunity to get a return on investment by transfer of such high-calibre people may not be so unlikely as it sounds, if the manpower utilisation business is to succeed.

OUTPUT VALUE

This relies upon the possibility of measuring individual or group output. The spread of work measurement techniques into clerical and managerial areas from manufacturing areas makes this sound like a real possibility. The state of the work measurement art is by no means fully developed and many line managers have not incorporated it into their schemes of management. Output value must be based on measurement, as must appraisal of performance against objectives, and as the general development in application of management techniques of this type gains momentum hopes for output valuation will rise. It can be done already in many departments and it may be an available starting point for many managers prepared to take it seriously and investigate the value of what they are in business to do.

Aspects of the underutilisation and lack of appreciation of the value of people will be developed in the following chapters of this book. The total problem is formidable but there is much the line manager can do about it at an individual level. It is of first importance if we are to pull out of recession.

REFERENCES

Cost-Benefit Aspects of Manpower Retraining, Department of Employment and Productivity Manpower Paper number 2, 1970.

W.J. Giles and D.F. Robinson, *Human Asset Accounting,* Institute of Personnel Management and Institute of Cost and Management Accountants, London 1972.

Hekimian and Jones, 'Put People on Your Balance Sheet', *Harvard Business Review,* January 1967.

2 Analysing the Work Situation

In developing a systematic approach to people as an investment, the starting point must be an analysis of the work situation. Businesses develop in various ways for various reasons, and the procedures in them which become well established are too infrequently the subject of inquiry or change. It is by no means unusual to hear the old reason for doing a thing – it has always been done that way – as an excuse for avoiding change. The decision to step back and look at the situation is seldom made although there may be a suspicion that it is needed. The temptation to let well alone, in the face of numerous other pressures related to immediate survival, can be appreciated. This has produced a growth area for management consultants, who can take an unbiased outsider's look at what is going on. Their basic starting point is questions such as 'Why does this business exist? What is its purpose? How does it operate in relation to this purpose? Is it achieving its purpose?' Many owners or managing directors are content to be judged by an end-of-year statement of profit and loss and have little concern for return on investment, participation in growth activities and diversification into other related fields.

Under these circumstances line managers can be forgiven

if they are unmoved by such ideas as getting value from people. The climate is, however, changing and it is now accepted that line managers' survival is very much related to their own ability to motivate staff and get the best out of them. The opportunity for change now presents itself and line managers must work out their attitude and approach to it, but they will often need help.

WHAT IS THE AIM?

The easy and popular answer will be: to make a profit. This means that the ingredients of the situation producing this profit will need to be examined. But before pursuing any analysis it is necessary to be familiar with the key terms to be used. These can be defined as:

(a) *Job description.* A broad statement of the purpose, scope duties and responsibilities of a particular job or position. This is sometimes called a position description.
(b) *Job analysis.* The process of examining a job to identify its component parts and the circumstances in which it is performed. The detail and approach may vary according to the purpose for which the job is being analysed – for example, vocational guidance, personnel selection, training or equipment design.
(c) *Job specification.* A product of job analysis, a detailed statement of the physical and mental activities involved in the job and, when relevant, of the social and physical environment. The specification is usually expressed in terms of behaviour – in other words, what the worker does (skill), what knowledge is used in doing it (knowledge), the judgement made and the factors taken into account when making them (experience).
(d) *Personnel specification.* An interpretation of the job specification in terms of the kind of person suitable for the job. The characteristics are often set out along the lines of the seven point plan (Chapter 4) or a variation of it.

The extent of this analysis and the amount of detail needed will depend upon the scale of the operation but it is inappropriate to embark upon the total without first conducting a pilot experiment by isolating a priority element of the work for special attention. The relationship between total and elements must be continually reviewed as findings about one will affect definition of the other.

COLLECTING INFORMATION ABOUT THE JOB

Suitable methods come under the following subheadings:

OBSERVATION AND INTERVIEW

This is an analysis operation covering the actual working situation. Description of the routines, procedures or approaches used would be followed by discussion and question. Identification of the input, processing and the output involving relationships with other individuals or departments will reveal overlaps and grey areas. The collection of this data requires a special kind of interviewing skill and the ability to identify paths of activity and the purposes for which they have been provided. Frequently the person doing the job will be unable to give reasons for particular activities and will simply be carrying out instructions without attempting to analyse. Jobs with a high discretion or decision content and little routine will exercise the skill of the analyst to the full.

A checklist would contain the following items: job title, number of people involved, the input of work, its source and its form, the process for distinguishing between routine and occasional tasks, points of decision and consideration available, responsibility for and to others, lines of communication and reasons for using them, equipment and facilities available and their utilisation, the output of work, its form, destination and standards. It is important also to distinguish between factors of the work which if unsatisfactory would lead to extreme dissatisfaction (hygiene or maintenance factors) and factors of the work which if improved would lead to extreme satisfaction (motivators).

This process of observing and inquiring will produce much information and it will also indicate areas for further inquiry, or analysis in greater depth, perhaps by different methods or different people. Interviewing groups in addition to individuals may offer a means of illuminating the dark areas.

WRITTEN QUESTIONNAIRE

This is desirable in two situations. First, where several people are doing the same type of job. To interview them all may be impossible but it may be necessary to seek different interpretations or confirmations, which can be accomplished by asking different people the same question on paper. Second, it may be desirable to explore special aspects of a task more carefully. The opportunity to think and then respond in writing may be a helpful discipline for the people concerned.

STUDIES FOR OTHER PURPOSES

Examples are work study or reorganisation for a variety of reasons related to flow of work and methods of payment (especially job evaluation). The ground may have been covered for reasons of this kind and the use of the information on a multipurpose basis will clearly add to the efficiency of the activity. Before starting a special analysis it will be advisable to check whether the information is available in another department if studies of payment systems and work study have been done before.

SOURCES OF INFORMATION

DIRECTORS OR DEPARTMENTAL MANAGERS

They will be more concerned with the total situation than the elements of it, as they should have delegated things of this kind to section managers or supervisors. An overview of the situation is, however, very desirable and the skilled analyst will have this in mind when framing questions and an approach to the detailed investigation. Where delegation is either misunderstood or rejected, opportunities to discuss or introduce it can be developed, which illustrates one of the fringe benefits of job analysis – the opportunity to discuss other management topics. In such discussions, of course, the basic topic of information about jobs must be kept in mind.

Many managers who embark upon this analysis will find themselves discussing jobs and, as a consequence, organisation for the first time. The confrontation with precise questions of this nature will require from them thinking of an unfamiliar kind. Directors or managers may find it necessary to analyse their own jobs before they can discuss the total situation, which may reveal to them some surprising information. Their knowledge of time utilisation will change as the facts emerge. They will undoubtedly find they spend less time on the important things, and more on the unimportant, than they had ever realised. There is no disgrace in this revelation, provided lessons are learnt from it.

Directors or managers who take this look at themselves, while looking at other people, will have cause to be grateful to job analysis for this self-knowledge. The further analysis of their own attitudes and 'funny little ways' may result in a quite unlooked-for self-understanding process. If directors or managers are to get maximum return upon investment from their employees they must be prepared also to give this maximum themselves. The whole operation may need a shake up – including the boss. It will be useless to attempt to analyse jobs which are disorganised or out of control unless it is accepted by those involved that the operation is intended to reveal or illustrate such a state of affairs. Where organisation and control are thought to exist and are found not to, the unintentional result of the exercise will be worth having.

The job analyst very often brings these sorts of unpleasant facts to light, and so the manager who accepts the need for job analysis has also to be prepared to tackle anomalies, faulty organisation, inadequate communication and lack of effective delegation.

SUPERVISORS

Although they are members of the management team, in fact the first level of it, supervisors will be closer to the mechanics of jobs and systems than the line managers to whom they are responsible. Where genuine delegation is practised they will have been given some freedom to organise and use staff in their own way to produce adequate section performance. If they have been set targets or objectives, it will be possible to measure personal effectiveness as revealed by the effectiveness of the section in relation to the total department. Whether or not this is the case, it is reasonable to expect the supervisors, no matter how hard pressed they appear to be, to know what the people in their sections are doing.

Unfortunately, there are still many supervisors who see themselves, and whose managers allow them to see themselves, as members of the working unit rather than members of management, and in times of pressure they will take their jackets off and do the work themselves, or resort to excessive overtime. This is always an indication of bad organisation, wrong allocation of work and poor management. One of the most difficult, and most discussed, questions of total management is how to bring supervisors into the management area and detach them from the day-to-day doing of jobs as they have always been done. They usually regard themselves rightly, as experts at the tasks of the section, which was probably one of the reasons for their promotion. They will probably be biased towards their own style and method, and expect other people to be doing the job their way when, in fact, they are not. If the supervisor can be involved in and given responsibility for seeking information about jobs as part of a total job analysis, it will be of real help to both the supervisor and the analyst. They both will gain understanding of precisely what is being done and how it is being done.

THE PERSON DOING THE JOB

Preparation for this stage is extremely important as there is every likelihood of hostility. To start asking people about their jobs and to investigate what they are doing without first understanding an operation or the reasons for it will be asking for trouble, and may perhaps lead to union involvement at the wrong time for the wrong reasons. There must be a careful initial explanation to individuals or groups of people concerned by either the line manager or the supervisor, or both together, of the reasons for the job analysis, its purpose and what may happen after it is completed. This explanation should never be left to the analysts, especially if they are from outside the business.

The amount of information that can be gained from co-operative employees is tremendous and they will often reveal things which were never previously known, problem areas which never rise to the surface and human relationships which cannot be allowed to exist. This vast supply of untapped information, which has been there all the time, is the contribution to organisation and efficiency which the people can make. Many managers do not realise that this information exists, or, if they do, they choose to ignore it. Managers and supervisors are always surprised to find how little resemblance there is between the way a job is being done and how they think it is being done.

THE LEAVING INTERVIEW

This is a much neglected source of information, for both the line manager and the personnel manager; it is full of promise as a fact revealer and should be treated as an opportunity not to be missed.

Though it may be too late to prevent useful people from taking their services elsewhere, it is not too late to find out why they are going. If leaving has given a person sufficient confidence to let the hair down, this presents a rare opportunity to really get the facts and there could be much constructive criticism available to managers if they are prepared to let it flow. If they can prevent the interview from degenerating into mud-slinging, and provoke suitable responses from the person leaving, they should learn what a job is like, what is going on, what are the personal relationships, what is the worker's view of management and what sort of improvement would be useful to improve and clarify jobs. The manager will need to listen carefully and should be prepared to sift out the useful from the useless.

EMPLOYEE REPRESENTATIVES

This has become more usual since the introduction of legislation, especially in the United Kingdom since 1975. The introduction of Codes of Practice, understood procedures and opportunities for participation either on boards or committees has provided a valuable opportunity for management to seek the views of employees, through their representatives, on work situation analysis. Such channels will be critical of the past, especially the work situation leading to unemployment, and the atmosphere may be emotionally charged. The need for skilful handling goes without saying or the positive possibilities will be submerged by negative attitudes. Changing the concern of employee representatives from survival to growth is a major management problem of the early 1980s.

Whatever the source of information, the person attempting to define jobs, investigate organisations and relationships will find there are stumbling blocks. The chances of success will depend upon the ability to:

- Explain convincingly why it is being done.
- Be specific about the value to be gained from it.
- Avoid injury to confidence, sensitivity and pride in those whose jobs are to be analysed. There is no suggestion that a person is incompetent or that work is unsatisfactory. The interest is centred on the job at this stage, not the person doing it.
- Convince that this is not the 'thin end of the wedge' leading to loss of jobs and redundancy but an analysis resulting from the quest for development, growth and profit to benefit all. It may be difficult to be convincing about this and it must be regarded as a major stumbling block to getting co-operation from those involved.
- Appreciate that it will take time and intrusion into the working day which will be unwelcome, especially in pressurised situations. If the investigator is positive and gets on with the job it will be to everybody's advantage. The time taken and the inconvenience will be reduced.

The analyst will need to be skilful to win the confidence of those he is interviewing, by designing his questions and regulating his approach to match the temperaments of the different people he meets. Upsetting people will jeopardise the project. Work analysts should be able to put themselves in the shoes of the person doing the job, in order to understand it, but they must not be deterred from getting the information by the unpleasantness or difficulties they meet.

PROCEDURE IN ANALYSING THE JOBS TO BE DONE

Line managers will not usually be the right persons to undertake this analysis themselves because:

(a) They will have neither the time nor the skill.
(b) They will be too involved in the total situation personally to be unbiased in approaching it.
(c) They will be unable to get the true facts out of people. Employees are often inclined to tell managers what they think they would like to hear rather than what is actually being done.
(d) They may be part of the problem themselves.

Collectively these reasons are good enough to stop the faint hearted in their tracks. The old-style managers, who are resistant to change, will succumb to this easy way out until change is imposed upon them by new higher management, possibly to their disadvantage. Managers of the future will be seeking help as a matter of some urgency, either from the company's personnel manager or from an outside specialist. To know about personnel objectives and principles is the managers' responsibility, and this knowledge will place them in a good position to keep up with the findings of the experts, challenge these findings and be a party to the decisions which must follow acceptance of them.

Managers in service industries often feel that analysis of jobs, setting objectives, improving productivity, motivation and performance appraisal are not appropriate for them. Nevertheless these concepts apply to all businesses, and perhaps more so in service industries where people are the major asset. Service-type work can be measured and productivity can be improved by better organisation of jobs and utilisation of people. It must also be appreciated that in all businesses there is an input, a processing and an output which must be identified in total before analysis of the components can take place. The key tasks, which are the major aspects of the job vital to effective performance, must be identified early in the investigation by the analyst.

Having settled these matters the analyst will want to examine the chart of the organisational structure, and he may have to start by compiling one. The absence of such a chart is a continuing source of surprise to outsiders looking at the management of businesses. Companies which have grown to the level at which they can become public frequently have no such chart, although their other assets, especially financial, will be very clearly tabulated.

The organisation chart will show how the work is broken into sections, identify the people responsible for them and clarify lines of communication. Analysts will continually be referring to the chart and will mentally modify it as anomalies are revealed. In their effort to get a true picture of jobs, they will certainly be content to compare it with reality in the initial stages rather than looking for likely changes. They find functional systems easy to follow as the work of a section will be concentrated on one activity – for example, purchasing of supplies. Flow organisations, where a person's job entails contact with different functions – for example, a designer who arranges supplies himself direct with representatives – will clearly be more difficult to understand.

Pin-pointing decision-making will not be easy. Frequently it is not clear how decisions are made. They often seem to happen rather than be the subject of controlled attention. Decision-making is a process which in general is far from being understood, especially in pressurised circumstances, and the need to distinguish between short-term decisions and long-term decisions, which involve principles and precedents, is not always appreciated. The chart is extremely important as part of the job analysis procedure.

The analyst will probably hope that the manager or supervisor will be able to provide a job description of some kind to serve as a point of reference in comparing the information and opinions he has collected. If it did not exist previously, it is not uncommon to find the manager and supervisor in disagreement about this basic information, especially if they are supplying it for the analyst. In many cases, however, getting this information will be just too difficult and no useful purpose will be served by getting bogged down at the beginning because of the lack of it. The analyst becomes accustomed to being faced with 'You tell me while I listen'. This is the first indication of the magnitude of his task.

The interview will follow a structured pattern, but deviations will be needed to explore the implications of what is being said. While recording information the analyst will need to filter out from it opinions, attitudes, feelings of a personal nature (such as frustration and jealousy), personal salesmanship (efforts to impress the analyst), chips on the shoulder and numerous other fringe contributions. These should not be dismissed, however, or taken lightly, as they may be of great value. To get a person talking freely is part of the technique. Fragments of the truth will be contained in all these things and the analyst who becomes irritated by them, or who cannot control them, will be missing much of value. A straightforward question and answer session will not usually suffice, and if it could a written questionnaire could be substituted. The essential information will be concerned with:

- Input and output from the section.
- Processes involved.
- Routines and standard practices.
- Areas of discretion.
- How queries, problems and unusual situations are dealt with.
- What are the priorities and the pressures.
- Contact with or dependence upon other people inside or outside the section.
- Administrative matters.
- Technical matters.
- Human and industrial relations.
- Standards and checks against these.
- Rejection of unsatisfactory work arrangements for rectifying it.
- Passing on instructions and information.
- Arrangements for training.

MAKING USE OF INFORMATION OBTAINED

It is now necessary to return to the starting point to reflect upon how information gained is to be used and to recall the desire to know more about the jobs being done.

The objective is to get the right people in the right jobs, giving full value for money invested in them. The starting point of this objective has been established as knowledge about the jobs, which must be gathered before any attempts are made to match people to them.

The job description has been criticised as a useless piece of paper consigned to the bottom drawer and never used. This could well be true, but only in situations where the motives for producing it are not understood and the need for it is not accepted. Like all management techniques, it requires management initiative and must lead to some action. The production of a piece of paper is the means to an end, not an end in itself. It is not the end product but the starting point of much beneficial activity. It is an action document having temporary value – it must be the subject of review and change as action produces change. Its purpose is to get more work done in less time, at less cost and of greater value so that all concerned may benefit from greater rewards. The actions will be indicated in the following directions:

(a) Reorganisation of the work into more appropriate sections with the elimination of time wasting, over-lapping activities, underutilisation of people, lack of control.

(b) The opportunity to cost and assess the value of the work being done as indicated by the cost and value of its component jobs. In its simplest form this will be a payroll check that will indicate cost and variation of cost with time as people are added or subtracted from the activity. The wisdom of adding cost by way of additional people, or by paying more, cannot be assessed without the understanding of value, and the relationship between additional cost and greater productivity, or increased value, must be measured.

(c) The identification of inappropriate or missing people in the structure. The age, skill, personality, experience and balance may be wrong and imminent crises, caused by significant retirements or possible resignations, can be allowed for.

(d) The need to recruit new people and to redeploy others. Specifications of skill, knowledge and experience can indicate the new blood required, while changes in the technology or the product can be anticipated before recruiting commences. Newcomers will reap the benefit of having their jobs understood and defined before they commence operations and they can be properly tuned in from the start.

(e) An indication of training needs both on the job and in general. Changes in technology or product will make it necessary to retrain existing competent staff to vary their contribution or change it entirely if they are to remain in employment and continue to bring value to the business. Changes in structure and in the organisation of work will produce a similar need especially for supervisors and managers. In the latter respect, the catching up needed for supervisors and managers who have received no management training at all, or who have been left hopelessly behind, will indicate a definite high-priority training need which may have to be tackled on a comparatively large scale.

Training for development and promotion will be built into this total look at the jobs situation in relation to the organisation chart. The thinking process associated with compiling it will enable an accurate analysis of the work situation to be made.

Having completed this cycle line managers will have at their disposal a wealth of information, and the onus is upon them to use it. They should also be contemplating the implications of it for their own jobs and their lives as managers. They cannot return to the situation as it was before they started the analysis, and having provoked indicators to change they must have the courage to implement them, especially when the changes affect themselves. In future, management – and particularly the management of change – must be based on knowledge and appreciation of value.

3 Sources of Supply

Whether analysis of jobs, followed by job specification and personnel specification, has been found necessary or not, the problem of finding the right people for a department or a business is a real one. Investment is involved as money is being spent on:

- Advertising or other publicity.
- Interviewing and other selection procedures.
- Induction or introduction of new employees to the work and the people.
- Basic job instruction, or training, using either off-the-job programmes, or on-the-job instruction by supervisors.
- Payments, other than salary, not recoverable if the employee leaves after a short time.
- Unproductive salary during induction and basic training.
- Interruption costs caused by the new employee making mistakes, asking questions and receiving on-the-spot immediate guidance.
- Training costs for instructors or supervisors giving instruction.

Obviously these depend upon the complexity, scale and frequency of requirement and attempts to cost are difficult.

The point, however, must be made that getting people into jobs requires an investment for which the manager must attempt to get a return, even if he feels it cannot be measured exactly.

PRIMARY SOURCE: INTERNAL

Before any person is added to the payroll it must be quite certain that the internal supply of talent has been fully utilised. Chapter 8 is devoted to the promotion and development of people but it is appropriate to apply its messages here. When a new situation arises, whether by resignation, promotion or transfer, all internal possibilities must be explored before a new person is engaged. This is a hard principle to follow in times of high unemployment, when most managers would like to create jobs, but the principle of job creation can only be applied where there is growth, or increase in productivity. To appoint new people without either of these will be to repeat the mistakes of the 1950s and 1960s and cancel out any gain in productivity achieved by reduction of the labour force in the 1980s. Line managers who have a vacancy justified by productivity must explore their existing resources and ensure that there is definitely no way of filling it by internal means. The advice of the personnel manager, and confirmation by other line managers that they do not have candidates for transfer, are the next stages. When all internal possibilities have been exhausted and no suitable candidate has become available, then, and only then, can external sources be used.

EXTERNAL SOURCE: THE EDUCATION SYSTEM

In large organisations, with full-time personnel and training staff, well-organised training schemes for young people and procedures for allocating them to departments following basic off-the-job training, (for example, industrial apprenticeship schemes), the managers are unlikely to be involved in the basic selection and training process. It is to be hoped that they will be aware of the company's programmes and be making a contribution to the identification of needs, content of training syllabuses and allocation to departments. They will, however, be away from the details. In small organisations, where such facilities are not justified, line managers will find themselves much more involved in recruiting and attracting into their departments or businesses suitable young people who are looking for their first jobs. For this reason, they will need to know the education system and appreciate that much has happened in it since they left school or university themselves. They will find an ever-changing situation where experiments, which may seem strange, are taking place. They will also have to recognise and adjust to the attitudes and outlooks of young people. The manner, appearance and motivation of these young people will be difficult to understand, especially when managers try to visualise them in their own work place.

Line managers must be able to cater for the needs of young people coming into working life, especially when they are in personal disagreement with them. Survival depends upon getting new blood into the business, which can be developed and taken advantage of because of these very differences. The young workers' strong points must be utilised by channelling each person into an appropriate job, and the managers must come to terms with the following inescapable facts:

- Young people now spend more years at school.
- They mature, and develop a will of their own, earlier.
- Styles and appearance are different and sometimes offensive to the older manager.
- Authority will be challenged and it will have to be capable of justifying itself in face of challenge.
- Rituals and customs will not be accepted.
- Dullness and boredom will provoke a quest for remedies.
- Standards of behaviour are different, which is not to say that they are lower.
- Ease of travel and availability of more money at an earlier age have widened experience at an earlier age.
- Teachers are different and so are teaching methods.
- The welfare state will provide and there is no feeling of humiliation about this.

– There is serious frustration arising from widespread unemployment.

These facts cannot be ignored and, when faced with them, it is more than likely that many line managers will have to change themselves rather than expect others to change. It is constructive to recognise the differences between the new and the old brigade and to create opportunities to turn these differences to advantage rather than to reject them. At the same time the business cannot be subordinated to or controlled by them. The point of compromise will exercise the ingenuity of line managers seeking to attract young people.

Line managers who are established in their departments and have become set in their ways will be out of touch with this requirement. Breaking through to change must feature in all management thinking and training, especially in relation to people, and in attempting to provide business continuity by replacing retiring older staff with younger people. The spread of collective bargaining and employee representation into all occupations, especially white-collar, is an additional important factor.

SCHOOLS

Managers should put themselves in contact with teachers and school leavers more directly. Ideally, a relationship should be developed between local companies (represented by personnel and training staff initially but by line managers eventually) and the schools. Efforts by staff of the Careers Advisory Service (formerly the Youth Employment Service) to inform school leavers about the type of job for which they are best suited, and what they will actually do in that job, have often been frustrated by lack of interest from industry and commerce. In larger companies part of the training manager's life is devoted to careers talks, exhibitions and provision of careers literature to schools.

The high unemployment situation in the UK, coupled with severe changes in the UK industrial training boards, have spread negative attitudes. Attempts to create jobs by the government, supported by grants, are praiseworthy but of only temporary help in bridging the gap between leaving school and starting work. Line managers have been too occupied with survival to be concerned about using the wealth of talent available (and decaying, as young people leave school to find there are no job opportunities for them). They cannot ignore their managerial responsibility for ensuring a continuing supply of suitably trained and skilled people. These people will be desperately needed as companies pull out of recession. As it is, companies will seek to strengthen themselves and are likely to find such people are not available. This source of supply is being seriously neglected and, whilst the reasons are appreciated, line managers should be looking at it positively and with an eye on the future.

UNIVERSITIES

The academically inclined children from public, grammar and comprehensive schools are the enlarged university population and managers should be hoping to benefit from this increased supply of young people armed with higher education. The ability to use highly academically qualified people in industry will depend upon the ability of managers to take the fresh look at their jobs advocated in Chapter 2. Graduates, who have experienced much difficulty in getting what they regard as worthwhile jobs over the past few years, are puzzled that such a state of affairs could ever exist. The over-assessment of national graduate needs by academics who are out of touch with industry is equally puzzling to industrialists, now being criticised for not providing jobs of the appropriate calibre, or any jobs at all.

Compromise will, of course, evolve, but line managers will find it necessary to take the initiative in looking at the jobs and redefining both their organisations and the jobs to take advantage of this abundant supply of clever young people. Any line manager who can work this one out has the opportunity to add good people quickly, if he will sort out his working situation with this in mind. Graduates will find themselves interested in jobs previously outside their scheme of life but offering opportunities to use their brains in organisation and business ways rather than academically.

This is important food for thought, as too many line managers take the view that these young people are too highly educated for their businesses, have inaccurate ideas about the length of time needed to become the boss and have inflated ideas about their value. These things may be true in relation to jobs as they are and have been for the past ten years, but the essential point to grasp is that line managers will need the brains, initiative and enthusiasm of these young people in the future. Managers may have to change themselves, their approach to work organisation and the jobs themselves if they are to avoid surrounding themselves with the mediocre and those motivated only by money who will leave to go elsewhere in quest of more money.

The world recession and the consequent economies mean there is a decline in higher education in the UK and this source of people will undoubtedly be variable in the future as the effect of economies becomes apparent.

BUSINESS SCHOOLS

As a source of supply, the business schools cannot claim that they have been numerically significant but they claim, with some justification, that their products are treated with suspicion by managers who give little consideration to them at departmental level, except in the very large organisations. This is an investment matter, as the two original UK business schools, formed in 1956 in London and Manchester, were financed initially by money from industry and commerce. There is a strong feeling amongst employers that although the business schools have attracted ambitious, high-calibre young people to invest up to two years of their lives in them, in many cases an unfortunate side-effect often appears in the graduates. This is associated with the employment expectations which business school graduates acquire which makes line managers see them as impatient, inexperienced people with big ideas who feel they should be quickly at the top. Line managers who can integrate business school graduates into their teams, give them controlled opportunities and a chance to show what they can do, will probably be surprised to find that such people can, in fact, get to the top quickly and take fresh air, new ideas and constructive change with them. This is a misunderstood source of supply in the UK and the line manager should make an effort to come to terms with it and make full use of it.

EXTERNAL SOURCE: THE LABOUR MARKET

A major growth industry since the early 1960s has been recruitment advertising. The national newspapers, professional and technical journals have all catered for it and an enormous source of income has become available to them. Allied to this, and perhaps a stimulator for it, has been the growth in availability and success of the selection consultant and the employment agencies. This sector has, of course, suffered in the economic decline of the early 1980s – in fact, it is sometimes regarded as an economic barometer.

Because recruiting on the open market is a difficult and expensive activity it should never be tackled by the amateur. It is a popular fallacy that anybody can recruit by using common sense; there is an expertise involved. If line managers need to use this source of supply they will probably need help in using it, but they should attempt to master the principles involved if they are to get the right kind of help and make maximum use of it. The help usually takes one of three forms:

(a) In larger organisations employing a full-time personnel manager, properly qualified to recruit, interview and select people, the need can be immediately satisfied internally.
(b) The services of an outside specialist, such as a management consultant, offering recruiting and selection as one of the consultancy skills.
(c) The services of an agency or the Department of Employment, via the appropriate register or job centre.

USING THE COMPANY'S PERSONNEL MANAGER

This service needs the following stages organised in accordance with company practice:

1 A job specification and a personnel specification docu-

ment, prepared by the line manager (perhaps with help from the personnel manager), submitted to the personnel manager in the form of a requisition supported by the appropriate authority from the line manager, departmental head or director concerned.

2 Assuming external recruiting, consider the sources of supply from which will follow the method or medium of advertising.

3 Compile the advertisement, deciding upon the style, layout, length, cost of the space and printing blocks.

4 If national advertising, place the advertisement through an agency or direct to the medium.

5 Analyse the replies, assessing suitability on paper; decide which ones to interview.

6 Conduct preliminary interviews and propose two or three candidates for interview by the line manager; arrange any special selection methods such as tests.

7 Interviews by the line manager either individually or with the personnel manager, followed by selection of the most acceptable candidate; this must rest with the line manager, and the personnel manager should advise on, but not impose, selection.

8 The personnel manager finalises all details, such as starting date, taking up references, induction course arrangements, letter of appointment in accordance with the requirements of current legislation.

The experienced personnel manager will be able to structure interviews and identify areas of a candidate's background which need more detailed information or analysis. It may be necessary to act as a tutor to the line manager who may be inexperienced at formal interviewing but will be looking for specific information about a candidate. Interviewing is often regarded as an easy activity for the inexperienced and a receptive line manager can learn much from a specialist by being present at an interview. Very often it is a case of knowing what is needed but not knowing how to get it. Framing questions capable of bringing out the needed answer, without making it obvious what this is, needs skill.

Companies wishing their line managers to take interviewing seriously and become competent at it, for reasons other than recruiting (perhaps performance appraisal), have found it necessary and worth while to provide in-company training for groups of managers or, in isolated cases, to make use of external courses such as those offered by the Institute of Personnel Management. Competence in interviewing is so essential to the job of management these days, and is used for many purposes, that it must form part of any management training course. As a manager's life is a series of human relationships, his ability to assess views and attitudes as well as facts is clearly an important one.

USING THE EXTERNAL CONSULTANT

The employment of an outside specialist is an established part of the recruiting scene. It is not confined to small companies without a full-time personnel manager, but is also made use of in many large organisations having the services of well-established and competent personnel specialists of their own. The reasons for this are well understood by those who use this method but they will not necessarily be clear to the line manager who is out of touch with the work of management consultants and who, in fact, may treat them with circumspection or suspicion. The reasons are generally thought to be as follows:

- Where adequate skill is not available in the company and where its permanent provision would be unjustified.
- Where there is some special feature of the appointment which requires a full-time concentrated attack on a difficult recruiting area, such as could not be provided by the personnel manager because of his involvement in a multitude of other personnel activities clamouring for his time and attention.
- For prestige purposes in attracting high-calibre people who are possibly reasonably well satisfied with their present appointment but who can be attracted to move by the consultant's approach on behalf of a company.
- For security or confidentiality reasons and in cases where the company wishes to remain anonymous, accepting that suitable people are unlikely to respond to a box number.

Commercial intelligence work is possible from the scrutiny of company advertisements for staff as are indications of weak areas.

- For convenience and time saving accompanied by a cost saving. Recruiting costs compare very favourably and the time taken is likely to be reduced for the important type of appointments usually amenable to this type of treatment.

The selection consultant's approach is based first upon his ability to understand and identify the key requirements in a situation, usually complex, and then by his ability to match candidates to these requirements. Success will be based upon adequate inquiry and assessment of the situations and the people with whom the person appointed would be in contact. Identifications of skill, knowledge, experience and qualifications is not too difficult – identification of style and personality frequently is. What would appear to be small personal prejudices about people, if they are not appreciated, can often waste the expertise of the consultant, and managers engaging a consultant to recruit senior people must be prepared to reveal these things if they are to get value for money. This approach is usually reserved for senior people whereas agencies have a record of success amongst the more junior ranks, especially in clerical, secretarial and accountancy appointments.

The consultant's method would be similar to that of the company personnel manager, including the job description, design of advertisement, analysis of candidates on paper and preliminary interviews, followed by presentation of a short list of not more than four possible candidates who match the specification as closely as possible. The client will then make a choice with guidance from the consultant if it is needed. Contact for at least a year after the appointment, to check the success of it, and perhaps help with any special unforeseen aspects as they arise.

USING EXECUTIVE SEARCH, OR HEAD HUNTING

This method, using personal inquiry and search techniques, is gaining in popularity and the line manager should be aware of it. Undoubtedly misunderstood, at one time regarded as unethical, now gaining in respectability and reputation, executive search has become an established method of finding the right senior people. It is based on the principle that the right person for the job is unlikely to see, or reply to, an advertisement. The most suitable candidates may not be on the market and are apparently satisfied with their present appointment. In these circumstances advertising will never succeed and these candidates have to be searched for or 'head hunted'. It is also effective in situations of shortage or scarcity, where the possible number of applicants must be small and advertising has little hope of producing the right candidates.

A certain mystique has grown around the activity, suggesting cloak and dagger methods, which is unjustified. It relies upon knowing where to look and being able to use the right approaches. It needs an information service, availability of contacts and a knowledge of how to develop and follow up possible lines of communication to places capable of revealing the right persons, or information on where they can be found. The approach is a personal one. The consultant will usually make contact with possible candidates by telephone indicating the purpose of the call and suggesting a meeting to discuss the matter. The recipients are at liberty to decline, following which it is unlikely that they would be pressurised in any way. They rarely decline as they have every right to be flattered by this selective approach and their natural curiosity will make a meeting a strong possibility. The matter is developed from there on a personal basis, but with similar stages to the advertisement method.

Success depends upon sources of information and the files of those engaged upon executive search contain much information about people and businesses without those concerned being aware of it. Much of this information is stored in a computer so that, to give an example, if the task is to find the best marketing director possible, information about such people influencing the world's most successful companies by competent marketing could be retrieved from it. Information is not gained by underhand methods but by analysis of sources like company results, the press, learned society or professional association activities, attendance at seminars and top-level courses, lecturing and writing.

It is confidently predicted by the enthusiastic advocates of executive search that it will become the normally accepted method of finding senior people and that it will replace advertising methods. The critics of the latter maintain that the best candidate can never be available, only the best candidate from among those who apply. Like all recruiting methods it can only succeed if managers or directors in search of people are able to be specific about their needs the more precise they can be the better will be the chances of specifying and finding the right person.

USING A COMMONLY NEGLECTED RESOURCE: WOMEN

The impact of women upon the labour market has increased at a phenomenal rate in recent years. Equality in education has been a foundation for it and opportunities for women in this direction should be on the basis of educational attainment. Although there has undoubtedly been discrimination against women in the world of employment, this is no longer the case in education, and women can expect to compete for top jobs. There are already examples of this in politics where there are women prime ministers, cabinet ministers and mayors; in medicine where there are women doctors and consultants; in law where there are women barristers; and even the London Stock Exchange has found it impossible to exclude women from the floor of its house. In the UK the Equal Opportunities Commission has worked hard in this area to impressive effect.

The old reason for not employing young women in career jobs – that they are likely to be available for a short period only before leaving to raise a family – no longer holds good. Women have demonstrated that they can raise a family and have a career at the same time. The pattern of having families early, then returning to a career, is established and is likely to become more prevalent. In general, whether males like it or not, the woman's place is no longer necessarily in the home.

Male line managers will find it necessary to reflect upon this situation as they will be increasingly faced with applications, for what would normally have been regarded as male jobs, by females who will often be better candidates. Whether he likes it or not, women are entering management and if the male manager wants to get the right person in the right job he cannot ignore the fact that the right person may be a woman. Legislation to ensure equal pay for women doing equal jobs is another factor underlining the value of women, and if women wish to compete with men for their jobs on an equal pay basis they will prepare themselves by acquiring skill, knowledge, experience, qualifications and outlooks which will enable them to do so. Women, like men, are sharing in the revolt against dull jobs referred to in Chapter 2, and the potential must be realised in the quest for value from employees. Women are a comparatively untapped resource available to line managers capable of getting it into perspective. The legal provisions in the United Kingdom for maternity payment and rights of re-employment are, of course, important factors.

These sources of supply exist and they are realistic. Properly understood and properly used, they will be the starting point of the right person in the right job.

REFERENCES

British Institute of Management, *The Business Schools,* 1971. A survey conducted for the Advisory Panel of Management Education for the Council of Industry for Management Education, known as the Owen Report.

N. Newman, 'The MBA Credibility Gap', *Management Today,* December 1981.

4 Selecting the Right People – I

Line managers who are not experienced in selection procedure view the activity with misgiving, often suspicion. When faced with a choice, from a number of apparently equally well-qualified and acceptable applicants, which should they choose? Many will feel that the final choice will be settled by the personal acceptability of a not so highly qualified person, rather than the high qualifications of a person who is not so likeable. This balancing of personality and qualification is one of the basic problems in selection, as the ideal combination of personality and qualification is rarely to be found in one person. There is, in addition, often a feeling of fear in the mind of a manager not accustomed to receiving new people into the department. This fear can be a stumbling block when an older person is faced with the prospect of controlling and getting maximum value from a younger person, more highly educated than the manager concerned, from a different background and having the attitudes already described in Chapter 3.

Line managers often find it necessary to seek expert help from outside, especially in recruiting senior people. The dangers of recruiting, when those involved are insufficiently experienced, are so serious that mistakes could put the firm out of business. In helping directors and managers to get these matters into focus, one of the messages of this book is they should not only recognise and become more effective in as many personnel areas as possible, but acknowledge that certain matters will be outside their scope and that help should be sought, on the basis of knowledge, rather than abdication of responsibility. In companies with a personnel department this may be the outside help required, but the manager, not the outside specialist, will always be the final decision-maker, both from the point of view of what is needed and being able to recognise it when it presents itself. The main dangers involved in recruiting people are:

- Inaccurate identification and description of the exact need.
- Wrong identification of the personal characteristics required – one of the biggest mistakes is to look for an exact replacement for a person who is leaving.
- Wrong identification of the right type of person on paper. Shortage of time to tackle this aspect conscientiously when faced with a large number of applicants (and it can take a long time) will lead to waste of time interviewing the wrong persons.
- Insufficient interviewing ability and experience, inadequate to cope with candidates skilled at being interviewed, able to maximise their strong points and minimise their weak points.

However, whether outside help is available, desirable or not, it is possible to give some guidance to directors and managers who accept that they should be more knowledgeable about selection. The situation is not hopeless and there are some principles which can be applied to most circumstances. Knowledge of these principles, and an interest in applying them, will not only enhance the prospect of getting the right person into the right job but will improve other aspects of good management which depend upon the ability to get to know employees and utilise them efficiently.

ADVERTISING

The principles of recruitment advertising, while having special features, conform to those of all general advertising. That advertising is expensive, and that value for money must therefore be a factor, go without saying. Nevertheless, the reader of the appointments columns in the national daily and weekend newspapers may be forgiven for wondering whether these considerations have been lost sight of. Irrelevant information and superfluous words not only waste space and, consequently, money but indicate lack of thought about the appointment, which will repel good candidates. The first principles are:

(a) *Attract attention.* The design of the advertisement – appropriate borders and division of headings and words, making use of the blank space, displaying company name or logo, style of type and size of the advertisement – can do much to attract possible candidates to read it. This is the first objective achieved; having attracted attention it must be retained and a desire to answer must be created.

(b) *Create desire to answer.* This is a selling operation so the benefits and attractive features must be covered accurately in an order of priority as follows:
  (i) Information about the company – such as what it does, where it is, what is the size and scale of its operation.
  (ii) Information about the job – detailing its ingredients and responsibilities, also its place in the structure of the firm and an indication of the future prospects.
  (iii) Information about the candidate – age, desirable background, qualifications and experience.
  (iv) The rewards of the job – salary and fringe benefits.
  (v) Information about applying – name of the person to write to, address and closing date if there is a time limit.

(c) *Stimulate action.* The style and wording require a special kind of skill, as overselling and flamboyance will repel and underselling will stimulate no response. Too many replies can be just as embarrassing as too few and will indicate that the specification has been two vague or general so that too many unsuitable people have applied. It can be argued that to receive two first-rate applications is better than a hundred second-raters. In some cases it is impossible to be as precise as desirable. For example, a manager wishing to attract one or two graduates with two years' experience since leaving university into his department as future management talent, will find it necessary to provoke a large number of replies to see what sort of people are available. Adequate time will have to be allocated for a serious analysis of the large number of candidates, on paper and at interview.

An example of suitable copy for an advertisement in recruiting a marketing assistant is given on page 45. In certain cases it will be undesirable to reveal the name of the company for reasons such as commercial or business intelligence or revealing information to competitors. Publication of a salary may sow seeds of discontent among existing staff, who may be receiving lower salaries for what they regard as equally important work, or threaten the salary structure of the entire department. There may be good reason for attracting a new person who is an anomaly in the existing salary structure, and provided that the manager is following definite policy, rather than letting this happen without noticing, there is no need to worry about it. The information may, however, have to be suppressed by an anonymous advertisement. To omit an indication of salary, as an alternative way round this, is to jeopardise the campaign since there is significant loss of response in such cases. The other possibility, use of a box number, cannot be advocated as the surrounding mystery is likely to put off candidates; people like to know with whom they are dealing. The use of a well-known recruiting consultant is often the way round these difficulties. A cheaper service is known as a 'post box' which will not reveal the name of the company but gives an address where there is a competent person to handle the matter. The names of any companies to whom applications should not be forwarded will usually be asked for.

MARKETING ASSISTANT

The Marketing Director of J Smith & Co Ltd, the well-established manufacturers of metal and plastic car accessories, needs a senior assistant. The company, under dynamic leadership, is expanding its business into Europe and is highly successful in the UK with turnover in excess of £10m a year.

The successful candidate will be responsible to the Director, with whom there will be a close working relationship. In addition to contact with customers, involvement in press and public relations activities will need an impressive style and pleasant personality to develop the company's image.

Ideal candidates will be graduates of about twenty-six years of age having at least two years' experience of the marketing function after completion of engineering training. A starting salary of £8000 pa will be paid and a car will be provided. Relocation expenses to the Midlands, where the company's headquarters is situated, will be paid.

This appointment is available to both male and female candidates, who should apply in writing to the Marketing Director, J. Smith & Co Ltd, Midtown.

ANALYSIS OF REPLIES

Although it will be useful and interesting to read letters of application and form impressions from doing so, it will soon be apparent that all the required information is not supplied.

A letter will always tell the reader what the writer wishes to reveal and means of gaining the additional information, upon which further progress will depend, must be found. The much-maligned application or career detail form is, therefore, unfortunately indispensable. The completion of this form is understood to be a tedious nuisance and is time consuming. A promising candidate can be put off by a four- or six-sided document which, when completed, will tell the story of his life. A well-designed form is, however, necessary at some stage of the proceedings, but if there is sufficient information in the letter, or if further progress can be made by a short telephone conversation, then the form can probably wait until the short list stage. On the other hand, a form may be to the candidate's advantage as it may help to establish with some certainty his suitability, or unsuitability, for the appointment. Serious candidates will wish to present themselves to best advantage and the form may bring out important information which has been forgotten in the letter or which just did not occur to the applicant. To get as far as an interview and be rejected is especially disappointing, and to be eliminated on the basis of paper information, in definite cases of unsuitability, is perhaps not quite so disappointing as after a personal meeting.

As applications have been invited in confidence, managers must spare no effort to ensure that this obligation is honoured. The grapevine is the most effective of communicators and leakage of information about applicants may cause untold difficulties for those genuinely attracted to another job for sound reasons but who cannot afford to upset their present employers. Impressions of the manager and the company are formed at this stage and it is as well for them to be good ones.

APPLICATION FORMS

As with advertisements, there are principles to be applied in designing and preparing application forms. They are in themselves a kind of advertisement for both the job and the company. Good impressions can be gained from concise, well-organised and businesslike documents; bad impressions from unimpressive, irrelevant and tedious pieces of paper. In organisations regularly involved in recruiting different types of people for different types of jobs at different levels it is likely that three or four types of application form will be needed as not the same details and emphasis will be required for, say, a designer as a filing clerk. The universal application form cannot be advocated. Good forms will contain separate sections as follows:

(a) *Personal particulars.* Name, address, date of birth, family details, state of health, interests, hobbies and community activities.

(b) *Education and training.* Particulars of school, college, university and postgraduate education, business school, professional or other qualifications and the method of gaining them, vocational training with particulars of any in-company or external courses attended.

(c) *Record of employment.* List of jobs in chronological order, giving the company, appointment held and responsibilities, the period involved, the salary progression achieved and a brief statement of the duties and the experience gained plus the reason for leaving. Space for a longer statement of the present or last appointment may be desirable, although this would be the subject of much discussion at interview.

(d) *Names for personal or business reference.* There are opposing views about the need for this information at this stage. To require applicants to seek the support of other people is suggested by the advocates of the requirement to ensure sincerity in making the application at all. The advocates say that since information will be required if appointment is to be offered, it is a good idea to get it at the beginning. The opponents suggest that this requirement, like the form itself, could deter some good candidates who do not wish to reveal their intentions to a third party at this early stage. However, the candidates would be willing, in fact expect, to draw upon support by way of references if they are to be offered appointment and the offer is subject to references. The value of references is doubted by many managers who feel that candidates are unlikely to give the names of people whose support would be unenthusiastic, with the result that references will always be good. It does, however, give access to other opinions and people prepared to give references are entitled to expect some guidance about the areas in which opinions are being sought. To invite an open letter will produce compliments and platitudes, rather like school reports. To ask a referee to comment on certain aspects of a person's career, life or makeup and for an indication of the circumstances under which the opinions have been formed, will help him to be constructive. Perhaps, after all, the best way will be to have a chat on the telephone. References are valuable, if they are thought about, and they often reveal features which would not otherwise have come to light.

(e) *Signature and date.* A signed statement, along the following lines at the end of the form, is recommended;

> I hereby declare that the statements contained in this application form, and any attachments to it, are to the best of my knowledge true and complete in all respects, and that no material facts have been withheld, misrepresented or suppressed.

ANALYSIS OF FORMS

Having analysed all the information on paper, three types of candidates will be identified:

(a) *Those clearly outside the specification for straightforward reasons such as age, inadequate examination performance, inappropriate experience, unrealistic salary ambitions.* In spite of the most specific advertisement capable of being devised there will always be a number of obviously unsuitable candidates 'having a go'. Polite, but firm, letters of rejection stating that there are other more suitable candidates matching the specification more closely than the person concerned should be sent immediately, at the same time thanking the candidate for applying and expressing regret that this is the case. There is no point in making enemies by an impolite brush-off, or worse still no reply at all; better to preserve the company image or enhance it.

(b) *Those clearly meeting the specification from whom further particulars will have been sought by sending them an application form.* Arrangements for interview are likely and these candidates may be sent a holding letter if dates cannot be arranged immediately so that they do not lose interest in the meantime. It is always advisable to keep in touch with interesting candidates and advise them of progress, delays and any other matters which if not made clear will tend to put them off.

(c) *Borderline cases.* Consideration of these would depend upon progress with those in category (b). They would be available if needed. After acknowledging them, indicating that there will be some delay, the particulars can be filed until the priority attention to category (b) has been exhausted.

PREPARATIONS FOR INTERVIEW

Successful interviews depend upon successful preparations. Time spent in structuring the situation, compiling a checklist of facts to be established, attitudes to be explored and motives to be understood, will be a worthwhile investment. The checklist approach to interviewing must not be rigid as the points must be covered conversationally rather than by question and answer. The candidate should be encouraged to talk and become relaxed.

Background information about the companies a candidate has worked for and influence upon them are important in senior situations. For example, the possibility of appointing a person as a financial controller who is from a company recently in financial difficulties must depend upon establishing beyond any doubt that he was not a significant contributor to disaster. There may be some difficulty in convincing a skilled interviewer of this, but if the candidate is strong in all other respects both sides would wish to be clear about this important point. This illustrates one of the most delicate aspects of interviewing, having to persist with the analysis of apparently unsatisfactory career features until the truth is established. It is easy and pleasant to discuss success, not so with failure.

As taking copious notes is neither possible nor desirable,

if interview continuity is to be maintained, some system of implementing the services of the memory will be needed. By setting out facts in a systematic way before starting the interview it is possible to annotate these or amend them so as to be understood afterwards as an aid to memory rather than a diary of the proceedings. Tape recorders can be used to preserve entire interviews and in some especially complicated cases this may be the solution, but it must never be done without the knowledge and consent of the person being interviewed. Its disadvantage is the time factor involved in playing back the tape and listening to it, which means virtually repeating the interview perhaps three or four times. Video equipment is now readily available and is increasingly being used to record interviews, especially for overseas clients.

In all cases an interview report should be compiled straight away, otherwise the first candidate will be almost forgotten after six interviews. A standard form is useful for this setting out the important matters either in prose or tabulated as a grading under certain headings.

At the risk of stating the obvious it must be said that the administration must be efficient and complete. Candidates must know the time and place of the interview, who will be the interviewer and that person's relationship to the job or the firm. The room must be prepared with adequate ventilation and there must be freedom from interruptions, especially by the telephone. The candidate must be put at ease and a relationship developed quickly to encourage communication. Barriers of tension and shyness, which are experienced by all people in interview situations, no matter how confident they normally are, must be demolished. After the interview arrangements to pay travelling expenses and information about the next stages of the application should be available. Impressions are still being formed and the details are important.

CONDUCTING THE INTERVIEW

As interviewing is a skilled activity managers who have never been taught how to do it, or who are short of experience, should seek training. It must also be re-emphasised that success in selection can only follow success in identifying a need correctly, so the job specification and personnel specification stages cannot be omitted. From then on it is a matching process, one of relating what the job needs to what the person is capable of giving. The matching of paper particulars will precede the personal matching by interview and a systematic approach has to be worked out. All individual interviewers will have different ways of setting about this but the line manager who is about to become involved seriously, either individually or with outside assistance, should be aware of the seven-point plan or a variation of it. This was devised by the National Institute of Industrial Psychology and it has stood the test of time as an aid to systematic interviewing for all kinds of situations. A booklet is available but to indicate the approach the following table of points is quoted from it:

1 *Physical make-up.* Are there any defects of health or physique that may be of occupational importance?
2 *Attainments.* What type of education, training and experience have been completed? How successful both educationally and occupationally?
3 *General intelligence.* What is the level of intelligence and what are the indications as to the extent to which it is applied?
4 *Special aptitudes.* Is there any marked mechanical aptitude or manual dexterity? What facility in the use of words or figures? Any talent for music and the arts?
5 *Interests.* To what extent are interests intellectual, practical, constructional, physically active, social or artistic?
6 *Disposition.* How acceptable to other people and how influential? Is the person steady, dependable, self-reliant, extrovert or introvert?
7 *Circumstances.* What are domestic circumstances? What do other members of the family do for a living? Are there any special openings available?

This plan cannot be regarded as a magic selector but as a valuable aid or discipline fitted into the interview situation. Some of its aspects would be of no interest in certain jobs but questions about them may help to reveal the total person. Whilst it divides the factors of interest into seven categories it does not seek to divide people into categories but seeks to help total understanding by isolating components which can be analysed or assessed.

As part of the matching process this plan will still depend upon personal judgement of what is being said, and interviewing skill is based upon being able first to extract information and second interpret it. A successful interview will much depend upon the preparatory work which is done. Merely reading through the application form will not do. It must also be remembered that the interview is a two-way communicating process and the applicant will be assessing the interviewer just as much as the interviewer is assessing the applicant. Time should always be allocated for the applicant to ask specific questions and take the initiative before the session is concluded. There is much to be learned from the type of questions asked and it is more than likely that motives, prejudices, ambitions and hopes will be revealed by the questions asked and the order in which they are asked.

SOME GENERALITIES

The following points will help the manager to make the most of the interviews:

(a) Get the candidate to do the talking in a controlled way on topics under your direction. Do not allow rambling off into personal salesmanship.

(b) Be informal but not familiar.

(c) Do not put words into the interviewee's mouth, do not ask leading questions where the expected answer, rather than the true answer, is revealed. Do not prompt replies or they will be yours not the candidate's.

(d) Aim at continuity, not a series of disjointed hops from one subject to another. A highly skilled interviewer may use this technique to deliberately catch a person off guard on points about which there may be some suspicion or confusion.

(e) Do not let the candidate interview you, until you give the opportunity in question time, but do not react against this too hastily as it may display the initiative you are seeking. The interview must stay controlled so that you can regain the initiative when you are ready to do so.

(f) First impressions are important but do not be too much influenced by them. Avoid the 'I knew as soon as the door opened' assessment.

(g) You are in the superior position but do not let this influence your behaviour. You are there to get information and an assessment, not to demonstrate your superiority. If it is quite clear that the job and the person do not match for definite understood reasons draw the interview to a close. Going through the motions is unconvincing and if prolonged will more than likely lead to unpleasantness or embarrassment. Indicate the way it is and why. Your decisiveness and your frankness will be appreciated.

(h) Be aware of body language, where gestures indicate what a person is thinking. Placing and movement of the body, especially the hands and eyes, can give a skilled person interesting information. Non-verbal communication by gestures, attitudes and even the style of hand-shake, should not be missed whilst interviewing. Line managers will find literature on the subject and the reference given makes interesting reading.

(j) Do not leave the situation vague when you have finished. Indicate where you will go from there and what is the time scale. If you are not ready to do what you said you would do within the promised time, let the candidate know what is going on. Mysteries will harm the good relationship you have built up and a good candidate may withdraw if there is uneasiness about things. If you appear to lose interest so will the candidate.

(k) Perhaps your need is greater than the candidate's. Although the interview is subjective it has to be acknowledged that it is one of the line manager's most powerful opportunities to make contact with people. Not only in selecting for employment but in appraisal of performance, handling grievances and disciplinary matters, training and giving instructions, the ability to get on to a common wavelength with the person concerned is a very valuable one. Many line managers find interviewing a pleasure when there are pleasant things to be said, a nightmare when criticism has to be made or when unpleasant matters have to be discussed. Telling employees their performance is unsatisfactory and that they will have to go is unpleasant. Getting reliable employees in the first place by good selection interviewing will make this unnecessary.

REFERENCES

Desmond Morris, *Manwatching,* Cape, 1977.
Alec Rodger, *The Seven Point Plan,* NFER Publishing Co. Windsor.

5 Selecting the Right People – II

Though interviewing is undoubtedly the most widely used selection method, it has its limitations and frequently the expert will resort to other techniques as aids in making the best selection. This does not imply that other methods can replace the interview, as even with the most sophisticated selection programme capable of being devised, the parties must meet some time and get to know each other by way of an interview or discussion. If additional methods are needed, it is unlikely that the line manager will be sufficiently aware of their uses and misuses to select and administer them himself and help will be needed. There should, however, be an awareness of the possibilities and some idea of the objectives and procedures involved.

This chapter is intended to give sufficient detail for the line manager to know what is being talked about by those called in to assist. If additional selection methods are found to be necessary it can be assumed that the situation is complex or that there is some doubt about the exact requirement. Nevertheless, the objectives must be in no doubt so that the additional selection aids can be properly chosen to simplify the task rather than add to its complexity.

The reasons for adding other methods to the interview

procedure may be related to any of the following situations:

(a) *Recruiting of young people* – especially school and university leavers. Interview alone leaves much to be desired unless the job is very straightforward, low-level and is not intended to lead to promotion. There is a strong similarity about the products of the educational system; the differences in their style, dress and manner do not help the older manager to conduct a satisfactory interview and establish the right relationship by talking. If prejudice exists, this must be eliminated by doing something else. Lack of experience in working situations makes it difficult to know what to talk about and there is a great danger of drying up before any real progress has been made. The generation gap often shows.

(b) *Identifying potential.* If a manager is looking ahead, beyond requirements for the immediate job, it will be necessary to try to measure potential and detect qualities of leadership – not easy to be convincing about in a talking situation. Past experience may not have provided opportunities to display talent of this kind. If it did, impressions of its success are difficult to form.

(c) *Aid to final choice.* When an advanced stage has been reached, following successful interviewing programmes, the manager may still be faced with a choice from several apparently equally good candidates. To avoid making a decision on very superficial factors, additional evidence is needed and some other activity must be devised.

(d) *Dealing with high-flyers.* Some jobs carrying immediate responsibilities, prospects of very rapid promotion to a high level with very attractive rewards, advertised deliberately to attract high-flyers will invariably produce applicants who are good talkers and respond well to interviews. Their ability to be interviewed is of a high order and they will quickly gain the upper hand with most line managers. The decision process may not have advanced much further than the letter of application which, of course, was equally good. Help will be needed as the interview can only take matters to a limited stage.

(e) *Doing something.* Much selection, in fact the majority of it, is done by talking. To produce a situation where candidates have to do something and are observed whilst doing it is a very useful variation and much can be learned from it.

(f) *Success with people.* The interview isolates a person and forces him or her to perform as an individual. This is unrealistic in relation to working life where involvement with other people is a certainty. To introduce a group situation allowing observation of behaviour with other people will help to assess this aspect of a candidate's make-up.

These are convincing reasons for additional selection methods. In fact consideration of them may make the line manager speculate about the value of the interview. It must again be emphasised that other methods do not replace the interview but supplement it. Any activity must be co-ordinated so that additional evidence is being accumulated.

TESTS

The justification for tests is that there is something which can be measured and to which numbers or gradings can be applied. As an absolute or comparative thing it is clearly of value to apply something concrete like a number to, or as a replacement for, a subjective category or grading based on opinion or judgement, both of which are fallible. Interviewers attempting to grade without measurements will be relying entirely on judgement following exchanges of words, which is successful up to a point after acquisition of skill and experience. It may also be argued that the third factor of the seven point plan, general intelligence, can be assessed very adequately from the educational record, without having to resort to an intelligence test. This may be true, if there is sufficient evidence available.

The statistical approach used by psychologists in the interpretation and discussion of test results may put off the line manager not conversant with these apparently highly academic techniques. This should not be so, as this approach is not essential in down-to-earth situations, where the tests simply enable measurement of some characteristic to be made, relate the performance of the individual in a standardised test to either that of the general population (or a specific section of it), and make a comparative grading from norms of performance.

As with interviews, preparatory work is necessary. To inflict tests upon unsuspecting candidates will produce a reaction that may not be favourable – some may refuse to take them if the reasons and motives are not made clear. For tests to succeed they must be seriously administered, time checked by stop-watch if the test requires this, and executed in standardised conditions for different candidates so that comparisons can be made. Explanation prior to the tests is imperative as they will be of no value if candidates do not take them seriously or decide they cannot be bothered with them. Interest must be created and the seriousness of them established in the candidate's mind. Tests cannot be administered by the inexperienced as they are safeguarded by supply restrictions and this is how it should be. Organisations such as the National Foundation for Educational Research in the UK will supply test material only to those qualified to use it after attending an appropriate course.

Line managers who feel that tests could be of value in their selection programmes will have to seek outside help in administering and interpreting them. Some large companies which are particularly interested in tests for school leavers, such as engineering apprentices, or on adult staff will have a qualified tester in their personnel department. This may make testing sound difficult and appropriate only to large organisations. This is not so and the value for money to be gained from adding this kind of activity to the selection of key people can be impressive for smaller firms as well. The case for more professionalism in selecting people for smaller firms is a strong one as the effects of mistakes are so much more important. There is less scope for movement of people and rectification of mistakes in such businesses. It is difficult for a manager to blame a newly recruited person for failure if the manager is the one guilty of the selection. The problem of unravelling this situation is a big one, affecting not only the business but the manager's conscience.

The critics of tests have powerful ammunition at their disposal. Each human being is unique and so whilst there is in each ground common to all special traits must not be lost in grading people. There are two strong criteria in fact:

1 Answers to test questions can be false especially in word tests which usually require a choice between three alternatives. Some candidates will follow a middle of the road route and play safe. Others will feel they can identify the hoped-for answer and will give it. It is, therefore, essential that the candidates should be left in no doubt that reactions of this kind are wasting everybody's time. Time spent on explanation and creation of the right attitude will make this criticism of tests less valid.

2 Tests measure individual traits and the measurement of such aspects of a person as powers of judgement, sociability, independence and so on do not measure the whole person. The sum of some parts is often different from the sum of the whole is the basis of this criticism. It is also suggested that the factors being measured are the obvious, conventional factors, whereas the important ones are the unconventional, such as originality, creativity, etc.

In assessing the value of tests the line manager will need to be satisfied that the scene is properly set for the test to be taken seriously and be sure that the traits to be measured are relevant in the working situation.

Having established that testing is a sensible activity it is now necessary to be clear about the personal factors that are suitable for analysis by testing. These can be divided into three groups:

INTELLIGENCE TESTS

Most managers will have taken intelligence tests at some time in their lives, although perhaps not since leaving school. Attempts to measure human intelligence have been extensive in all parts of the world and have engaged the attention of psychologists, educationalists and sociologists in considerable depth. Experts have puzzled at length over the relationship between intelligence, intellectual capacity and performance in a job, and there is much literature on the subject. Unfortunately, little of it has found its way into management practice.

The line manager will be interested in intelligence as a foundation for, and indicator of, performance in a job. Though it may be thought that an 'intelligent person' is needed, it may not be clear which elements of the job will be tackled more successfully because a person is more intelligent. The ability to produce ideas, be creative, make deductions and proposed changes may be associated with intelligence in the manager's mind, but there will still be confusion about the relative importance of intelligence, knowledge and experience. Intelligence can also be regarded as a factor in decision-making, where collecting information, working out implications, drawing conclusions and advocating action leading to change are important. If there is a need for intelligence of a reasonable order, let it be measured.

Examination results as an indicator of intelligence are far from infallible: the relationship between intelligence, acquisition of knowledge, reliability of memory and ability to pass examinations is not well understood. Intelligence is not the same thing as learning ability. Learning ability is not an indicator of adaptability to new situations and problems; it does not necessarily influence motivation, speed or rate of development. It does indicate a capacity to approach difficult matters from first principles and the ability to reason and deduce.

A distinction between verbal and non-verbal intelligence is made in the design of intelligence tests and this may be done in the working situation. Geniuses grappling with tremendous scientific problems are notably inarticulate and can express themselves better in mathematical terms or diagrams than in words. Non-verbal tests can be expected to indicate ability to observe, deduce, work out, draw conclusions and then make a decision to take the right action. Tests using sequences of patterns, diagrams and objects eliminate verbal aspects of intelligence. So much work has been done on intelligence tests that the level, or norms, of performance can be accurately determined. In well-established tests these norms are continually up-dated by the addition of further test scores for appropriate samples of the population.

APTITUDE TESTS

The line manager will have no difficulty in appreciating that information about aptitudes is valuable and can be related to jobs. Mathematical aptitude in a performance analyst, manual dexterity in a typist or assembler of intricate parts, and an aptitude for visualising mechanisms in a designer are clear examples. The experts have often tended to distinguish between tests of aptitude and achievement, suggesting that aptitudes might be regarded as natural, inborn, and producing gifted children whereas achievement follows from learning with or without natural gifts. Music and painting are often thought to be natural rather than acquired. Point 4 in the seven-point plan is concerned with this.

In reality aptitude will develop with achievement and perhaps be improved by it; consequently aptitude as a pure thing in working life is difficult to be precise about. The manager may be clear what he means by skill but he will welcome help in recognising or measuring it, whether it is a natural or an achieved attribute. The area containing skill, aptitude and achievement will appeal as one capable of benefiting by test assessment. The most widespread use of aptitude tests in industry is in the selection of engineering apprentices. Here well-proven test batteries are available for school leavers and many industrial trainers are qualified to administer them. Two- and three-dimensional visualisation tests are also popular for prospective designers.

Aptitude tests would seem to be only marginally appropriate for adults, where aptitude and achievement may be clear from the employment record. There is, however, an urgent need for such tests in businesses faced with retraining programmes for older workers displaced by redundancy, or in building up new businesses in redevelopment areas where the skills available in the area are not right for the new business. There would be a need to recruit a number of such skilled workers for retraining in a different skill if they have the necessary aptitude.

Tests are of considerable value in deciding which candidates will be worthy of the investment the company will be making in them. This is a comparatively new possibility for tests of aptitude, brought about by rationalisation of businesses and the sorting out of manpower needs. It may well provide an area of future research to validate procedures in circumstances when stress or emotional aspects could be an important influence upon test attitudes and performance.

Research over a number of years has tried to relate special aptitudes to different occupations, such as nursing and piloting aeroplanes, but progress has been possible in limited directions only. It has been especially disappointing to those engaged in vocational guidance work when people possessing natural abilities, which suit them for a particular occupation, do not wish to take up that occupation. In the times of indiscriminate addition of people to the payroll, aptitude was replaced by other considerations, which makes research upon this subject impossible. A desire to appoint only people having the right aptitudes for the work would have prevented many misfits becoming established in work to which they were basically unsuited, only to be shaken out later. Aptitude tests can make a significant contribution to getting the right person in the right job, if management is prepared to take them seriously and spend time identifying the skills which are of importance.

Skills analysis, when combined with work study and methods of analysis, is introducing a more scientific approach not only to the organisation and flow of work but also to the description of jobs and people doing them. If the total work situation is broken down into its elements, management is well on the way to identifying aptitudes which can then be the subject of selection tests. This applies equally to shop floor productive areas and to offices, and work measurement in identifying skills for the first time. In fact, before total productivity can be improved it may be necessary to give priority to office and service departments rather than concentrating the attack as usual on the productive departments. Improvements elsewhere can drain away in non-productive departments where organisation, analysis and identification of skills have never been the subject of serious attention.

Aptitude testing can be an ingredient in improving the whole business and as such will take its place on the list of investments destined to have a useful return.

PERSONALITY TESTS

Most managers will feel that they know about personality. After their management experiences at different levels in different situations they will feel they have met all the types and be able to recognise the extrovert, the studious, the conceited, the irresponsible and the co-operative. They may be accustomed to judging their staff for performance appraisal purposes on these very factors. Nevertheless, these judgements are subjective not only with regard to the personality being assessed but to the personality of the assessor.

Life is a series of encounters in which people find it necessary to estimate factors such as friendliness and dependability. These qualities are basic and dictate the nature of relationships with people at home and at work. They are distinct from intelligence and aptitude but are definite qualities which have encouraged psychologists to give attention to the measurement of them. Though personality is a total thing it cannot be investigated in total and so separate individual characteristics or traits have to be investigated.

Personality is related to situations, and personality tests seek information about how people react to situations and circumstances as they meet them. Groups of people can be compared on the basis of these traits which identify them as types. Tests of this kind are usually called inventories where a response is sought to questions about behaviour towards and feelings about an inventory of objects, people and situations. Other tests, classified as projective techniques, depend upon response to stimuli, such as ink blots or pictures projected on to a screen. The former will be more attractive to line managers who want to measure personality as they will understand the inventory factors, and might even be persuaded to take the test themselves.

A well-known example of the personality inventory using a questionnaire is the Cattell 16PF which seeks to analyse the respondents under sixteen personality headings or factors. Each of the sixteen factors is rated on a ten-point scale, and then a profile is plotted. The test is intended for adults over seventeen and it has variations for people of a higher educational standard than the general population. Each factor can be taken in isolation if a full assessment is not needed. Descriptions of the factors of the ten point profile scale are given in Figure 5.1.

These factors are self-explanatory and their investigation is growing in popularity. Managers will find it less and less satisfactory to rely upon their subjective judgement of people as they recruit again for growth after the recession and so will need to be aware of the help available from appropriate tests.

From Figure 5.1 it will be noted that there are extremes of grading, termed low score and high score for each of the sixteen factors. After marking and application of norms to the test result a profile can be plotted (see Figure 5.2), which gives an interesting picture of the person concerned. Departures from the average are clearly indicated. It will be seen that there is an indication of intelligence as one of the factors. Objective evidence of this kind, when considered in relation to subjective information, adds significantly to the line manager's knowledge of employees.

TEMPERAMENT TESTS

A new test available in the United Kingdom has enabled remarkably accurate assessment of temperament to be made. In 10 to 15 minutes it is possible to get very worthwhile evidence. It has been found especially useful in the selection of marketing and sales staff who need a selling temperament in addition to the basic intelligence and training required. In such cases if the temperament is wrong, no matter how adequate the intelligence and training, effective sales people will not result from the selection process. The first reference at the end of the chapter applies to this word survey test of temperament.

	LOW SCORE DESCRIPTION	HIGH SCORE DESCRIPTION
1	*Reserved,* detached, critical, aloof	*Outgoing,* warm-hearted, easy-going, participating
2	*Less intelligent,* concrete thinking	*More intelligent,* abstract thinking, bright
3	*Affected by feelings,* emotionally less stable, easily upset	*Emotionally stable,* faces reality, calm, mature
4	*Humble,* mild, accommodating, conforming	*Assertive,* aggressive, stubborn, competitive
5	*Sober,* prudent, serious, taciturn	*Happy-go-lucky,* impulsively lively, enthusiastic
6	*Expedient,* disregards rules, feels few obligations	*Conscientious,* persevering, staid, moralistic
7	*Shy,* restrained, timid, threat-sensitive	*Venturesome,* socially bold, uninhibited, spontaneous
8	*Tough-minded,* self-reliant, realistic, no nonsense	*Tender-minded,* clinging, over-protected, sensitive
9	*Trusting,* adaptable, free of jealousy, easy to get on with	*Suspicious,* self-opinionated, hard to fool
10	*Practical,* careful, conventional, regulated by external realities, proper	*Imaginative,* wrapped up in inner urgencies, careless of practical matters
11	*Forthright,* natural, artless, unpretentious	*Shrewd,* calculating, worldly, penetrating
12	*Self-assured,* confident, serene	*Apprehensive,* self-reproaching, worrying, troubled
13	*Conservative,* respecting established ideas, tolerant of traditional difficulties	*Experimenting,* liberal, analytical, free thinking
14	*Group-dependent,* a 'joiner' and sound follower	*Self-sufficient,* prefers own decisions, resourceful
15	*Undisciplined self-confident,* follows own urges, careless of protocol	*Controlled,* socially precise, following self-image
16	*Relaxed,* tranquil, unfrustrated	*Tense,* frustrated, driven overwrought

Figure 5.1   The ten-point profile scale

LOW SCORE DESCRIPTION		STANDARD TEN SCORE (STEN) → Average →	HIGH SCORE DESCRIPTION
RESERVED, DETACHED, CRITICAL, ALOOF	A	7	OUTGOING, WARMHEARTED, EASY-GOING, PARTICIPATING
LESS INTELLIGENT, CONCRETE THINKING	B	9	MORE INTELLIGENT, ABSTRACT-THINKING, BRIGHT
AFFECTED BY FEELINGS, EMOTIONALLY LESS STABLE, EASILY UPSET	C	8	EMOTIONALLY STABLE, FACES REALITY, CALM, MATURE
HUMBLE, MILD, ACCOMMODATING, CONFORMING	E	5	ASSERTIVE, AGGRESSIVE, STUBBORN, COMPETITIVE
SOBER, PRUDENT, SERIOUS, TACITURN	F	7	HAPPY-GO-LUCKY, IMPULSIVELY LIVELY, ENTHUSIASTIC
EXPEDIENT, DISREGARDS RULES, FEELS FEW OBLIGATIONS	G	4	CONSCIENTIOUS, PERSEVERING, STAID, MORALISTIC
SHY, RESTRAINED, TIMID, THREAT-SENSITIVE	H	4	VENTURESOME, SOCIALLY BOLD, UNINHIBITED, SPONTANEOUS
TOUGH-MINDED, SELF-RELIANT, REALISTIC, NO-NONSENSE	I	5	TENDER-MINDED, CLINGING, OVER-PROTECTED, SENSITIVE
TRUSTING, ADAPTABLE, FREE OF JEALOUSY, EASY TO GET ALONG WITH	L	3	SUSPICIOUS, SELF-OPINIONATED, HARD TO FOOL
PRACTICAL, CAREFUL, CONVENTIONAL, REGULATED BY EXTERNAL REALITIES, PROPER	M	2	IMAGINATIVE, WRAPPED UP IN INNER URGENCIES, CARELESS OF PRACTICAL MATTERS, BOHEMIAN
FORTHRIGHT, NATURAL, ARTLESS, UNPRETENTIOUS	N	5	SHREWD, CALCULATING, WORLDLY, PENETRATING
SELF-ASSURED, CONFIDENT, SERENE	O	2	APPREHENSIVE, SELF-REPROACHING, WORRYING, TROUBLED
CONSERVATIVE, RESPECTING ESTABLISHED IDEAS, TOLERANT OF TRADITIONAL DIFFICULTIES	Q_1	2	EXPERIMENTING, LIBERAL, ANALYTICAL, FREE-THINKING
GROUP-DEPENDENT, A 'JOINER' AND SOUND FOLLOWER	Q_2	7	SELF-SUFFICIENT, PREFERS OWN DECISIONS, RESOURCEFUL
DISCIPLINED SELF-CONFLICT, FOLLOWS OWN URGES, CARELESS OF PROTOCOL	Q_3	7	CONTROLLED, SOCIALLY PRECISE, FOLLOWING SELF-IMAGE
RELAXED, TRANQUIL, UNFRUSTRATED	Q_4	8	TENSE, FRUSTRATED, DRIVEN, OVERWROUGHT

(Reproduced by permission of the Institute for Personality and Ability Testing, Inc., Champaign, Illinois, USA. copyright © 1956, 1970, 1972, 1973 and 1979

Figure 5.2 The Cattell 16PF test profile

GROUP SELECTION METHODS

So far the discussion of selection has been confined to individuals in either face-to-face meetings or in individual tests. This is itself artificial in relation to the working circumstances, which are generally those of a group. People in groups, the behaviour of individuals in groups and the behaviour of groups in relation to individuals are topics for research. Behaviour analysis and behaviour-changing courses have become numerous recently as the popularity and usefulness of this study has grown.

In selecting the right person for the job it will be necessary to take account of the candidate's acceptability to the working group, not just to the managers responsible for the selection. This is a two-way business, as the result will be equally serious whether the group reject the individual or the individual rejects the group. The personnel manager, or outside consultant, working for a manager must treat this as a major concern. The armed forces recognise the group as essential to the assessment of leadership, resourcefulness, co-operativeness, team spirit and strong management. To place an individual in a group and watch performance at a given task is very revealing. It is equally revealing to watch the members of the group and their response to authority.

A selection activity using groups has developed in popularity. As with all tests it needs efficient organisation and stage management, also staff capable of running it and assessing it. More than one assessor will be required and the optimum group size will vary from six to ten, as control of a bigger group is difficult. Assessors will be concerned not only with the personal behaviour of individuals in the group but with such things as the abilities to introduce ideas and sell them to the others, to change track and still be constructive when proved wrong, to argue positively but not stubbornly or resentfully and to remain logical when emotions are aroused. There are two useful approaches to group selection.

THE GROUP DISCUSSION

This verbal exercise is rejected by some as yet another talking situation, well suited to the talkers of this life.

Though this is true it may effectively demolish the talker if his contribution is of little value. The procedure is simple and amounts to seating the candidates round a table, giving them a topic to discuss, without appointing a chairman, letting them get on with it and observing what happens. Experience indicates that patterns of procedure and behaviour emerge and tend to repeat themselves with different groups. The ready talker is likely to dominate at first, later to be suppressed by a quieter, deep thinker who has been marshalling his thoughts.

New ideas and thoughts will be introduced as the discussion gains momentum. One person will say virtually nothing and will be content to listen, another will be provocative, another will be the comedian, another the bringer back on to course. Apart from being very useful this is an entertaining and enjoyable selection aid, throwing up quite valuable information about behaviour in a group. Again, like tests, this is not a substitute for the interview but an additional provider of information.

THE GROUP TASK

It is possible to get away from talking by devising a group task where those involved must achieve something tangible. The task need not be related to the business with which the manager is concerned but should be capable of being tackled in different ways. Some may be sceptical of the value of using building bricks or constructional toys but such things are frequently used very successfully. To confront a group with a selection of bricks and ask them to construct a tower of maximum height at minimum cost when given information about the considerations involved is both interesting and informative. As with the group discussion reactions will differ and it is more than likely that the leaders and the followers will be separated and identified during the completion of the task.

GRAPHOLOGY (ANALYSIS OF HANDWRITING)

This interesting aid to assessment is more common than is sometimes realised. Its development has been stimulated by the need for additional guidance about highly personal factors, such as:

- Integrity
- Relationships with others
- Reaction to situations
- Regulation of behaviour
- Team spirit

It is, however, not an area for the amateur. There are experts available to managers and the possibility of seeking and using such further evidence provided by graphology should be considered.

The additional aids to selection discussed in this chapter are all tried and tested ones and have been found to be of value. Testing, setting group tasks, or graphology can be extremely helpful, but only if the manager knows the purpose of the exercise and what factors are important. They fit into the central aim of describing the right person and providing the means of finding that person with some reliability, but they are not for the amateur. Experts should definitely be consulted before using aids of this kind.

REFERENCES

McQuaig Institute of Executive Development Ltd, *The Word Survey* (particulars from the author).
UK National Foundation of Educational Research, *Cattell Sixteen Personality Factor Questionnaire* (Cattell 16PF) (available only to qualified test administrators).
Fraser White, *Key to Graphology,* W.H. Allen, London, 1977.

6 Matching People to Jobs

Describing jobs and seeking the right people to do them can be considered as two different activities, perhaps requiring different skills, but line managers must appreciate that success will only follow after a careful matching operation. On the one hand, they must be clear about the job requirements, and on the other, they must be equally clear about the sort of person they are looking for. Sources of supply, and chosen method of attack in finding the person, will be of little value unless the matching problem is understood and allowed for.

Although line managers may be happy to work at their jobs in the company, they should not deceive themselves into thinking that it will be natural for other people to join them just because they are offering employment. Many line managers feel that choice is all on their side but it is very much a two-way business, and it is by no means unusual for managers to be turned down by the person they want. When an apparently attractive offer, at a competitive salary has been refused, managers can find themselves asking why they were not able to make an appointment after the most careful, well-organised and sometimes expensive recruiting and selecting campaign. The explanation lies in the matching aspect of the situation and a failure to recognise that two questions have to be answered and understood: why people work and why people work for you.

Even in times of recession, when unemployment is high and there appear to be many suitable people on the market, the initiative often rests with the job seeker not the job provider. In such circumstances line managers are often baffled by the lack of appeal which they appear to have and by the fact that in spite of high unemployment there are unfilled vacancies. It must be realised, especially at executive level, that many highly capable people, redundant through no fault of their own, have to reappraise their situation, survey the market and consider possibilities of starting their own business, and will not be inclined to jump at the first job which comes along. The factors discussed in this chapter are of no less importance when there is high unemployment. In fact, often they are more important, since people released from a company because of the recession will look very carefully at a new employer and make every effort to ensure that the experience they have just passed through will not be repeated in their working lifetime.

WHY PEOPLE WORK – MOTIVATION

Most people work because they need to earn money. But money does not explain why some people do the jobs they do when they could get more money by doing other jobs, or why some people work to full capacity while others do the bare minimum they can get away with.

The subject of motivation is very topical and it must be accepted as a high priority for management in the 1980s. It is part of an approach to both general and personnel management that involves the application of the behavioural sciences to working situations. As is so often the case in management matters, this is an import from the United States but it has gained momentum in other parts of the world. Though the literature on motivation is extensive, the manager, for whom this book is written, may appreciate a summary of its principles and ideas.

Research conducted by Professor Herzberg and others in

the United States has demonstrated that in the working situation there are certain aspects of the job and the environment which, if below a certain standard, will lead to extreme dissatisfaction. These are called hygiene or maintenance factors. Other aspects, which if introduced or improved would lead to extreme satisfaction, are called motivators. All these aspects may be grouped together and summarised as:

(a) Salary
(b) Security
(c) Status
(d) Satisfaction (job)

The first two are normally regarded as factors which could lead to extreme dissatisfaction and are maintenance factors. The second two are normally regarded as factors which could lead to extreme satisfaction and are motivators. There are no rigid boundaries between them and while some people are undoubtedly highly motivated by money, others are equally motivated by job responsibility leading to job satisfaction. An important principle to bear in mind is that it is useless to try to motivate people if the maintenance factors are below standard. It is difficult or impossible to motivate by improving job satisfaction if there is no security in the situation and the salary is inadequate.

Maintenance factors are not a substitute for motivation matters and motivation is difficult, perhaps impossible, where maintenance matters are neglected. This is an important distinction which many managers are not clear about. To get the idea into focus managers should try listing their own motivators and maintenance factors, then ask themselves if they are motivated, or merely maintained, in doing their own jobs. It is a very important exercise as part of the matching approach which is advocated for application to other people. It is useful to elaborate a little on the four basic aspects grouped above.

(a) *Salary.* This can be more widely interpreted as reward. Not only the actual reward but the approach to deciding what it is will be important. Chapter 9 deals with this important aspect in detail.

(b) *Security.* This is considered by many as an obsolete concept. Managers themselves, now among the most insecure of employees, will have their own doubts about it. In many workplaces there is an atmosphere of living on a day-to-day basis, which is unfortunate and is a cause of discontent. Nevertheless, arrangements for sickness and accident as well as retirement cannot be neglected and will, undoubtedly, be dissatisfiers. Certainly, older workers will be concerned, especially those who do not believe that the state will, and should, take care of security matters. People are still anxious to cater for themselves and many highly motivated workers want to do so.

(c) *Status.* This refers to the signs of being considered important to the job and the business, of mattering, being cared for or belonging. Sir Walter Monckton, a distinguished Minister of Labour, referred to this a long time ago in the following words:

> No matter how good may be the technical equipment, however advanced the method or process, efficiency is in the end determined by the extent to which you have been able to cultivate a good team spirit within the unit. It is the feeling of oneness, the identification of the individual with the group, which gives life to all the techniques and policies.

This is a status consideration which makes people feel good, want to do more and do better because they have been noticed, want to grow to greater importance by doing more important work. This is working status.

(d) *Satisfaction* in having achieved something, having done something not only interesting to the individual, but worth doing and important to the unit. Satisfaction leads to development, or growth, in a situation receptive to growth, where the contribution of those motivated by the opportunity to make it will lead to a more profitable business.

It is imperative for managers to be aware of these matters and have organised thoughts about them, not only in abstract terms but as things that do apply in their own working environment and to their staff. It will not, however, help the matching operation under consideration merely to acknowledge them and hope that they exist. Some positive managerial action will be called for.

Appreciation of motivation is often jeopardised by line managers who think it can be applied in a general way. While the maintenance factors may be built upon a common foundation, motivators certainly will not. Different people will be motivated by different things, and different amounts of different things. Techniques for getting the best out of people depend upon an understanding of these matters and the subject of human relations and its relationship with getting the best out of people is, at best, vague in most managers' minds.

HUMAN RELATIONS

The ability to understand and regulate human relations is fundamental to effective management. Line managers will have to cross the bridge between an understanding of why people work and an understanding of why people work for them by accepting the importance of competence in human relations. The things to be clear about are as follows.

(a) *People are emotional* – rather than logical and rational. An individual's reactions to events are often shaped by temporary emotions, either personal or generated by a group. It is often possible to observe how the behaviour of a normally rational individual becomes completely irrational because of group or crowd influence. For example, some of the spectators at football matches, throwing missiles at the goalkeeper and abusing the referee, are usually quite normal, even meek and mild people. This out-of-character behaviour is caused by the emotion or pressure of the immediate situation. People often admit that their behaviour during an event was illogical and declare: 'If I had my time over again I would not have said, or done, that.' This sort of behavioural change may be obvious when stated, but line managers must realise their own liability to emotional change. They will find from reflecting back upon their own behaviour in pressurised working situations, and in trying circumstances, that they too act emotionally at times.

It is important to realise and take account of this in deciding a course of managerial action, and assess what will be the reaction of the people affected, especially if they are in a group at the time of conveying the decision to them. The example of a shop steward playing upon the emotions of a mass meeting, stirring them up to action, then damping them down, is not only well known but can be observed on television, which is an ideal medium for the study of human relations. Behavioural developments, especially in groups, can be observed whilst they are actually happening. In discussion programmes the interaction of different outlooks, styles and points of view can be watched.

(b) *People are prejudiced* – as a result of their own background. The reasons for this can be traced to family, educational, religious, political and social origins, all of which contribute to the complex makeup of every individual. These factors not only affect a person's past but will shape his or her future ambitions and desires. In looking at human relations to get the best out of people, line managers will find themselves acknowledging and trying to make allowances for matters of this kind if they are to succeed.

There are so many recent examples of personal and industrial conflict which stem from inappropriate action, or inaction, in relation to moods, attitudes and prejudices. These are, admittedly, complex areas of human interaction but the future will require management competence in dealing with them. Recognition and interpretation of them will enable managers to prevent or dissipate feeling of resentment or opposition to change when it is accompanied by suspicion.

(c) *People need encouragement and incentives* – also criticism when they are at fault but supported by guidance and leadership to do better. The old grumble about managers being quick to criticise but slow to praise may have been true in the past but in the future, when appraisal of performance will become a much more widely understood activity (see Chapter 9), the reasons will have to disappear. Incentives have been traditionally financial but a change over to incentives founded upon interest, growth, development and motivators will figure in management thinking.

The extent to which managers should know their employees will depend upon their own attitudes and the extent to which they believe it is part of their job and their desire to get the best out of people. The belief that it is possible to know the working capabilities of people without knowing them as individuals is held by some. Managers will have to go below the surface and be concerned about any aspect of a person if it affects performance on the job. The matching operation is very much dependent upon this knowledge and there are three reasons for this:

1 To establish a satisfactory working relationship containing mutual confidence and respect.
2 To know what kind of treatment will bring the best results.
3 To judge what knowledge, ability and personal qualities are available for consideration of development and promotion.

Getting to know people is an extension of the interview situation covered in Chapter 4, using an approach destined to reveal attitudes, prejudices and desires to people they already know up to a point. Managers who are good listeners put people at their ease, take an interest in what is being said and can be impartial and base their judgement on the evidence rather than on personal prejudices. If they are not over-influenced by isolated unfavourable actions, possibly out of character, they will have a chance to improve their human relations with existing staff. They will have to be prepared to allocate time to it. They may need to attend a human relations training course, exposing themselves to group feelings and so-called sensitivity sessions, which will help them become more competent at this difficult aspect of their jobs, especially the matching of people to situations.

Too many managers, immersed in their day-to-day problems, have not been able to give themselves a chance in the human relations field. In fact, their experience of human relations is often confined to conflict or trouble situations, which are themselves generated by inattention to human relations. These experiences give them a very jaundiced view of the whole subject as they associate it with trouble rather than working harmony.

Getting the right people in the right jobs, and keeping them, will depend upon skill at matching in human relations aspects; therefore, more skill must be acquired. Feelings are contagious and the manager's own feelings can easily be conveyed to his colleagues. Inadequacy, apathy, enthusiasm, aggression, humility and the habit of shifting the blame on to somebody else are common in managerial human relations. Efforts to become more effective will benefit from attention to the following:

(a) Self-criticism first: examine your own attitudes and idiosyncrasies.
(b) Respect the other person's feelings, especially self-respect. To damage this accidentally is bad, to do so intentionally can be acceptable provided the reasons are valid and the approach under control.
(c) Let the pressure drop and return to it later.
(d) Remember the differences between people.
(e) Try to put yourself in the other person's shoes. Understand the situation into which you are introducing your ideas.
(f) Appeal to positive feelings.
(g) Be sincere and radiate your sincerity.

The expression 'I know my people' is often used and it will be useful for managers, in the light of the subjects which form the basis of this chapter, to ask themselves whether they really do. The matching operation will depend upon the degree to which it is true.

WHY PEOPLE WORK FOR YOU

It is not difficult to appreciate the principles relating to maintenance factors, motivators and human relations but applying them in management situations may not be so easy. There are always pressures to tackle apparently higher priority matters, but the difficulties attached to the human aspects will increase if the wrong people are in the wrong jobs. Matching the right people to the right jobs is a factor in reducing managerial pressures and should not be contributing to it. Managers must find time to examine the maintenance factors and the motivators.

As with job descriptions, it is no use trying to apply new thinking to inefficient organisation, doing jobs the wrong way and jumping from one crisis to the next. It must be beyond doubt that the processes of the business are necessary, are organised properly and are understood. The relationship between job descriptions and matching people to the jobs is a close one and if the exercise has been completed for one purpose it will be available for the other. The answer to the question why people work for you is contained in this matching process. The person's needs must be satisfied by the job's requirements and this is the equation that must be used.

PEOPLE'S NEEDS

Another aspect of behavioural science which has attracted attention recently is the analysis and classification of individual needs. If Herzberg is the expert in motivation then Maslow is the expert in the needs of individuals. He has introduced the concept known as 'the hierarchy of needs' based on the idea that once a need has been satisfied it is no longer a need. This means that people will tend to produce another need as soon as the previous one is met. The hierarchy utilises the following steps, which have been used in helping to solve the needs equation:

- Physiological needs: food, clothing, shelter.
- Safety needs: security, order.

- Belonging needs: love, affection, identification.
- Esteem needs: success, self-respect.
- Self-fulfilment needs: achievement, growth.

These are a variation on those previously used, but it means that people will only stay in jobs if they are satisfying needs and if they continue to satisfy their developing needs as they move up the hierarchy list. Some people will have their needs completely satisfied before reaching the top of the list; others will need to go the whole way. If people are going to work effectively, the managers must be aware of their hierarchy of needs and make it possible for these to be satisfied in the job provided. If they are not, employees will look for satisfaction elsewhere.

TURNOVER

This lack of attention to the satisfaction of human needs is at the root of the turnover problem. Research has indicated that money is not the main reason for high turnover and that paying more money may be a short-term solution: the immediate need having been satisfied, the turnover will resume and continue to grow. The condemnation of jobs as dull, repetitive or routine is justified in many departments where jobs grow more dissatisfying as work volume increases and more dull work is heaped on to existing dull work. While it is accepted that there may have to be 'hewers of wood and drawers of water', analysis of dull office and operative-type jobs is long overdue if matching of people to jobs is to be a possibility. The vicious spiral of dull jobs leading to high rates of turnover leading to payment of more wages is no solution and has produced the anomaly of clerks doing dull and simple jobs receiving higher wages than, for example, hospital nurses.

The attitudes of those managers and supervisors who are not prepared to look at jobs from the point of view of satisfying needs and enriching them are major contributors to the problem. All jobs are amenable to some form of enrichment. It is a serious human relations problem, as to treat people as part of the machinery will lead to disaster.

This is not to say that every person must have the job enriched. Clearly many people are highly suitable for, and quite happy doing, dull repetitive jobs and the reason for this is that their needs are satisfied at an early stage in the hierarchy. Such people would be as unhappy if their jobs were enriched as a person with greater needs would be doing their job. The key here is the understanding of needs and the arranging of jobs so that they satisfy the needs of those doing them. To step back and take a fresh look at all jobs, especially the dull ones, is a fundamental necessity of management. If management neglects it, the unions will do it for them.

THE MATCHING PROCESS

Some final thoughts on matching are again related to the job description which identifies the following four components still of interest for matching.

(a) *Knowledge.* Starting with education, both full and part-time, knowledge gained in working elsewhere, from leisure activities, social and recreational. Efforts to increase the supply of personal knowledge by private study, reading or contact with people. These must be taken account of. There is a knowledge matching need.

(b) *Skill.* While knowledge may be both general and specific to a job, skill is usually related to a job or category of job. But other skills, such as writing or speaking, possibly acquired outside work, may be of value. There is a skill matching need.

(c) *Experience.* This implies the passing of time and familiarity from having done something repeatedly, or at least once before. Total experience will include that of life, perhaps enabling the formation of opinion or judgement, perhaps the ability to make good decisions, which will be valuable knowledge to any manager who knows which of his staff possess special experience. There is an experience matching need.

(d) *Personality.* This will follow from greater interest in human relations. It will be shaped by background, family environment and way of life. It will be the foundation for developing interest and growth and will strongly influence the motivating factors. There is a personality matching need.

So it is now possible to be specific about the components of matching.

- What does the job require by way of knowledge, skill, experience and personality?
- What does the person need, and what is that person capable of contributing, by way of knowledge, skill, experience and personality?

Managers who can balance these two sides of the matching equation will be getting nearer to having the right people in the right jobs and keeping them there.

REFERENCES

F. Herzberg, *The Motivation to Work,* Wiley, 1959.
F. Herzberg, *Work and Nature of Man,* Staples Press, 1968.
A. Maslow, *Motivation and Personality,* Harper & Row, 1954.

7 Introduction to Jobs

Attracting the right people into the business can be expensive. Recruiting costs nowadays are substantial and the investment in them must be appraised. Advertising and travelling expenses, plus the cost of the time used in getting and processing applications, can add up to a considerable sum of money but, surprisingly, few companies attempt to cost the operation. If an outside organisation or agency is used there will be no confusion about this as the bill will be there for all to see. However, the manager who is anxious to get value for money out of his recruiting activities will have to be concerned not only with getting the right people but retaining them. The various aspects of this are being discussed in this book. No matter how attractive the long-term future with a company, if the new employee does not survive the first few days, weeks or months then the activity has been futile and financial loss, as well as ill-feeling, have been incurred.

It is the manager's responsibility to give all possible attention to the first few days of new employees' life with the company and all possible attention to the new employees will help them to settle in and begin to feel that they belong. The sooner they can become effective, as full members of the team, the sooner its profitability will be influenced by their presence.

INTRODUCTION OF SCHOOL LEAVERS

The period of transition between leaving school and becoming a productive worker is, undoubtedly, one of the most difficult periods in life. To leave the well-understood routines of school life, after being immersed in them for at least eleven years, to join the world of work gives a considerable jolt to any young person. It is accepted that young people mature earlier than they used to but to believe that sixteen year olds are really nearly adult is often to be deceived by appearances. Youngsters' fashions and styles can lead the older manager into estimating maturity wrongly. The problem is not helped by those young persons who, especially if they are not handled properly by the manager, get a chip on the shoulder when they realise that work they thought would be easy is not. Here the human relations skill is critical and it has been discussed in Chapter 1.

The successful introduction of young people into business cannot be just hoped for or allowed to happen. It must be planned and handled in an appropriate way, taking account of the basic differences between the old brigade and the new. Much valuable work is, of course, being done in the schools and by the Careers Advisory Service, but much of it is by talk rather than involvement. Appreciation courses for school leavers in their final year have attempted to rectify this, but in too many cases good schemes have failed because of unsympathetic attitudes by industrial and business managers not prepared to co-operate and unwilling to allow young people into their departments to see what it is like before they make decisions upon their jobs and careers. This possibility has been around for many years but it has not become established practice in spite of the obvious need for it. The pressure on a manager's time is great but there is, undoubtedly, much scope for this kind of helpful activity without it being the disruptive nuisance which many claim it to be. The daily affairs of the department have to go on.

University graduates, who can take advantage of long

vacations, can take the courses which many of the bigger firms offer, although it has recently become more fashionable for them to consider voluntary service overseas, or physically challenging activities based on overseas travel. Many managers will say that vacation courses of the traditional kind can show little by way of positive results, or even evidence that they have served a useful purpose in either recruiting or introducing participants to work in general. In such cases managers can only blame themselves as usually the undergraduates have been used as little more than odd-job labourers or office helps. Clearly this possibility is repulsive rather than attractive and managers in firms of all sizes need to give thought to some positive action, to the problem of selling their jobs, their firms and themselves to today's highly educated and critical young people. Introduction to working life need not wait for the first few days but could commence before they actually start work.

It may be felt that this is taking the manager into fringe areas, more the responsibility of local authorities and educational establishments than industry. This is true, up to a point, and the manager will be right in feeling that it is just as much in the interest of the educators to concern themselves about the value of their education to the community and the employers, as it is for the manager to be concerned with it. After all, the community and the employers pay the bills.

Managers are openly critical of some educational ideas and priorities these days. They aver that although the educational establishments appear to be lavishly equipped with aids and have more time in which to do their job, the end product is not noticeably better. Many managers of small engineering firms envy the facilities in some school and college workshops where the machine tools are more expensive and more modern than those in the factory. They also comment upon the lack of competence in the basic skills of reading, writing and arithmetic which they detect in the products of the educational system. In the face of what is often hostility, because of factors like these, it has been found difficult, even impossible, to solidify a relationship between industrial managers and those responsible for education and careers guidance. Both sides understand these feelings but the onus has to stay with the manager, whose survival may depend on getting the right young person into the right job. The more enlightened managers will accept that the problem is theirs and will tackle it, overcome their own prejudices about the educational system and integrate valuable young people into the working team.

This problem of attitudes, especially in the young, has been aggravated in countries suffering high employment during the depression of the late 1970s and early 1980s. Large numbers of young people have found themselves out of employment from the day after leaving school. This is a social as well as an employment problem and it undoubtedly produces discipline and behaviour problems as well as anger and frustration. Helpful attempts to reduce the magnitude of this problem have been made in the United Kingdom by short-term training and job opportunity schemes. Unfortunately, line managers who can eventually employ these young people will find their capacity to be tolerant and understanding stretched to breaking point. In developing countries the problem will be similar when young people with the benefit of more education and greater enlightenment than their parents become employed in growing businesses in their countries, often controlled by expatriate managers.

The pre-employment period is not under the managers' sole control but from the first day when newcomers arrive, eager to get started, the total responsibility is theirs beyond dispute. This has created the need for and development of a process usually known as induction. In view of the problems discussed its importance at the present time is enormous.

INDUCTION OF NEW EMPLOYEES

This is an age of words and the industrial vocabulary is continually being expanded to include new uses for old words. Induction is one of these and the dictionary indicates that it relates to a process associated with installing, leading into or introducing, and it is, therefore, reasonable to use it in this context. In thinking about it the line manager is moving into what is often a training area, as it is usual for the company's training manager to be responsible for it in an overall way, and in particular from two points of view:

- Introduction to the firm, its systems and its people
- Introduction to the actual work

Line managers who can draw upon a specialist, such as the training manager, will be relieved of the basic conception, planning and organisation of induction courses, but they will be expected to become personally involved from the time new people are within the boundaries of their departments. Whilst it is acceptable for managers to delegate aspects such as the conducted tour of the department and introductions to the staff, to a supervisor, if they can find the time to do this personally they will be starting their relationship straight away and will not give the impression of remote figures who cannot find the time to take an interest in new people. The makings of a barrier may begin here and the greater the amount of the induction responsibility that is delegated the more difficult it will be to demolish this barrier.

Induction is an acute problem in departments faced with the turnover problems already discussed, and in extreme cases the manager may be faced with a succession of newcomers on a one or two-week basis. Proper induction can never happen under these circumstances, which will be an added factor in the vicious circle relating to turnover. Neglect on the first two or three days will lead to the newcomer's absence on Friday being interviewed for another job, and the addition of one more to the turnover statistics on the following Monday. In happier circumstances, especially when several newcomers start on the same day, or where there is an intake of school leavers, the company's training or personnel manager will have the opportunity to be systematic about induction by dividing it into three parts:

GENERAL INDUCTION TO THE FIRM

This includes reference to the firm's handbook, description of the business, how it is organised, who are its key people, traditional practices and maintenance of company standards. In situations where induction is a frequent activity, for example in building up workers in a new firm in a redevelopment area in stages over a year, it may be sensible to place much of this information on a programme either in machine or book form to ensure standardisation and increase its efficiency. In such cases the presence of someone will always be essential to introduce the programme and put a face to it. The process of feeling welcome, of belonging and of being cared about starts right here, so far as the company is concerned, and the individual begins to identify with the company.

DEPARTMENT INDUCTION

Although specialists would be expected to help with this aspects, in a variety of ways, this responsibility rests fairly and squarely upon the shoulders of line managers. As well as being personally involved they should bring their section heads or supervisors into it so far as their own sections are concerned. This does, however, mean that the section heads must be capable of doing this and, if necessary, have had some instruction about its purpose and the way to handle themselves. It is an important aspect of the supervisor's job and should be included in the training programme for supervisors. They cannot just be left to get on with it as best they are able whilst the manager adopts an out of sight out of mind attitude. The supervisor is a key man in induction as this is the newcomer's first point of contact with management. It is where the day-to-day involvement will take place and where human relationships must be cultivated. The seeds of discontent will be sown here and managers who appraise the performance of their supervisors will have this matter of induction on the list of things to be appraised.

The ingredients of a relevant induction course have been briefly described, indicating a divided responsibility between the line manager and the personnel or training manager. Inevitably there will be grey areas between them and it will be as well to recognise this, then make attempts to lighten them before they become an additional factor in the turnover problem.

The success of introducing people to jobs begins with the specification used for recruiting purposes. The type of person, and standard of knowledge required, must be clearly understood and the person selected must match this requirement as closely as possible, as the best induction course capable of being devised will never satisfactorily introduce the wrong person to the wrong job. Similarly, lack of basic education or knowledge will produce the need for a special pre-induction course and, while this may be necessary especially in jobs or parts of the country where appropriately prepared people are available, it must be understood or it will provoke irritation and conflict. In such cases the most suitable method of dealing with this will be to plan for it off the job, either in the company's training centre or any room, even a part of the canteen, which can be set aside for the purpose at certain hours of the day when it will be free from interruptions. There must be adequate means of checking that the programme is being followed, is succeeding and is continuing to be relevant. Checking the standard reached and the need for extra training or refresher courses will form part of this. Making certain that new employees are sure about their job responsibilities and that they are not worried about their capacity to do it is contained in this checking.

A clear distinction between company matters and departmental matters should be established to avoid obvious overlaps and omissions. The line manager must not be burdened with general company matters which should be covered by the personnel manager in the general induction programme or in the company handbook. The latter document is often conspicuous by its absence and line managers may find themselves having to promote such an idea to the board as an aid to proper induction of people into the firm. This need not be an elaborate glossy booklet; a leaflet which is expendable when it has to be up-dated is adequate. In general the need for such a document in a firm of any size is a very strong one. As an additional supplement to the individual contract of employment it can be extremely useful in stating, or clarifying, very general company matters not needed in every individual's personal contract.

JOB INDUCTION

This is a second induction responsibility for managers and

supervisors. Basic instruction will usually take place on the job and the procedure has generally earned the title of 'sitting by Nellie', which is derogatory, in many cases rightly so. There is, however, no escape from what should be more respectfully described as personal job tuition and there is nothing wrong with sitting by Nellie, if Nellie is a capable instructor, has been properly trained to instruct and is motivated to the task. Both the manager and the competent on-the-job instructor will be sensitive to such factors as nervousness, noisy surroundings. They will be aware of the value of illustration instead of talking and encouraging the asking of questions as aids to avoiding wrong work. The steps in the procecure are:

1 Explaining the job elements.
2 Describing each part and the reason for such a part.
3 Doing each part whilst the supervisor watches followed by constructive criticism and further instruction, or explanation, of points in doubt.
4 Controlled increase in responsibility, the rate of which will depend upon the individual.
5 Reporting back to the manager at recognised stages about progress followed by personal contact started by the question 'How are you getting on?' This should not be in the formality of the manager's office and the skilful manager will know how to contact people 'accidentally on purpose' at their place of work, when they are relaxed. People should not be summoned to the office.

LINE MANAGER'S RESPONSIBILITY FOR TRAINING

Managers who reflect upon their responsibility for getting new people off to the right start in their department, feel that they have attracted the right sort of people and are, consequently, anxious to retain their services, will accept that employee situations are never static. A readiness to review these on a regular basis will be necessary. This aspect of management is the subject of Chapter 8, but it cannot be completely detached from consideration of introducing people to jobs. Whether there is a training manager or not, line managers will have to sort out their attitudes to the training of their people not only during the introductory period but throughout the subsequent career. There are two major aspects to this responsibility:

- Assessing the training needs.
- Providing the facilities for and carrying out the training.

A departmental plan or chart showing the nature of the human resources, probable movements of staff, allowance for promotions, resignations and retirements will be needed, plus information about who has been trained to do what and how long ago.

ASSESSING DEPARTMENTAL TRAINING NEEDS

Managers who are practising contemporary management principles will be concerned about objectives, performance analysis, profitability and the need for change. Departmental controls will indicate how their activity is progressing. Though they will be concerned about day-to-day personnel matters, such as shortage of the right type of people, and labour turnover with its attendant wastage, it is to be hoped that they are looking at the future as one of the company's planners. If so they will know about their role as change agents and not only as a satisfier of immediate needs. This makes it necessary to avoid treating the induction of new employees as a steady ritual which will take care of itself. The first point of change may be in the induction of new people who will be facing different pressures and challenges to the supervisors who are changing them.

The need for a change will have to be instilled into those developing newcomers and into changing attitudes towards introducing new people to their jobs. To do something because it has always been done that way is the worst possible reason and managers must pass this message to supervisors by expecting change and provoking it themselves. This line of thought must exercise the manager's mind and rule the approach to the total training problem, of which induction is the starting point. It will often indicate individual training needs as it will not necessarily follow that the needs of one will be the needs of all. It will be the beginning of a continuing process, and a positive analysis of induction courses and their results by means of it will provide valuable clues for development which might otherwise be difficult to find.

Training needs always exist but the ways of identifying them are not always obvious. Often there is only a feeling that all is not well, where a deliberate search to find the cause will not be rewarded. It will be necessary to take advantage of all departmental activities as identifiers of training needs and induction is an outstanding example of an opportunity not to be missed.

INDUCTION AS A STAFF APPRAISER

The most expert exponent of scientific selection methods and highly organised recruiting procedures will admit that there must always be an element of chance in the selection of new employees. Some further admit that the first six months in a job is part of the selection process. After exercising the maximum amount of care in relation to the acceptable investment in recruiting and selection of people to match accurate information about the job requirements, opportunities to assess the procedure must be looked for. Many selectors look at long-term survival and promotion of a business as proof of their ability to get the right people in the right jobs, but they often turn a blind eye to their many short-term failures, indicated by the statistics of people leaving within the first year of employment.

Another factor to be included into the induction course design is the opportunity to weed out misfits who have slipped through the recruiting and selection procedures. Those concerned, whether the full-time personnel manager or the line manager, need feel no embarrassment about this as there will always be an element of subjective judgement in the decision to engage a person. Judgement is influenced by prejudices (discussed frequently in this book), and so inevitably mistakes will be made in spite of the most sensible and careful recruiting arrangements. The role of the induction process as a check on the selection process is an important one and when it reveals misfits, wrong attitudes, insurmountable deficiencies in skill, knowledge and experience action will be required. No induction course can completely overcome bad selection.

It does not follow that mistakes will always be on the negative side and it is more than likely that from time to time induction will reveal people who are too good for the job in mind. Potential or previously unrevealed qualities must be seized upon when they are revealed and up-grading, following an induction course, is just as urgent as weeding out and rejecting. The search for talent has to be intense and continuous. The success of this outlook in induction courses has to depend upon an unusually efficient system of communication between those selecting and those inducting. The gap which normally exists between personnel staff and supervisors responsible for induction is too wide to be bridged in most businesses. The attitude of the supervisor who tries to hang on to a new man who is clearly too good is understandable but cannot be tolerated in relation to the total business.

Supervisors who suffer in silence in the face of bad selection have only themselves to blame when faced with overloads, bottlenecks and substandard work because of having accepted, without investigation, the wrong people into the section at the end of the induction period. There will be plenty of opportunities to comment upon selection during induction courses and whilst in charge of on-the-job training they must make the most of these opportunities, in collaboration with the manager, to ensure that there is feedback of information to the recruiter, and that they are getting good service from him. It may, of course, be the manager who is at fault.

An additional responsibility rests on those in charge of the induction procedure in those countries where dismissal of employees is complicated by legislation. In the United Kingdom, for example, termination of employment after one year, for whatever reason, can be challenged as 'unfair dismissal'. In such disputes the induction programme will be in the spotlight since a company which cannot demonstrate effective induction may be judged against in an industrial tribunal, who can order the offending company to reinstate the employee with additional training or pay compensation.

INDUCTION AS A COMPONENT OF ON-THE-JOB TRAINING

Formal induction at company and departmental level need not take very long – it may last a week, it may last a day. Departmental interest will frequently begin seriously when on-the-job training starts. It is appropriate to emphasise the unusual opportunity this presents. While it is taking place there is a close relationship between two people, the supervisor and the new employee, which may never exist again. This close relationship can be very valuable but it is often so neglected that its value must be stressed at every opportunity and it must be taken advantage of when it arises.

In subsequent job situations the responsibility of the individual is frequently masked or hidden by the influence of other jobs and other people so the manager finds it difficult when responsibility for success or failure needs to be pinpointed exactly. In the case of failure, where it is usually possible to blame materials, other processes or other people for set-backs, it is even harder to get at the truth. This difficulty of isolating the individual is what makes appraising people at all levels so hard, either for salary review or performance. Information about and impressions of new people when their work is controlled and checked by a competent supervisor or instructor, as in an on-the-job training situation, can be of great value to the managers in getting to know new people. If managers can develop self-discipline by taking notes and keeping brief records of these matters they will be protected from the inevitable loss of this accurate and substantiated information with the passing of time. An opportunity like this may never occur again.

INDUCTION AND RETRAINING OF REDUNDANT WORKERS

The recent widespread rationalisation of businesses and

pruning of staff numbers has produced, on the one hand, much human misery and, on the other hand, a supply of talented people for those businesses able to employ them. People squeezed out of their jobs, perhaps after as much as thirty years' service with a firm, have every right to feel rejected, unwanted and the victims of all kinds of misfortune. Many will never find jobs of equal calibre to those lost. Many will never get jobs in the same type of business again. They will have to adjust to a new occupation at an age beyond that in which this is usual and regain their confidence as quickly as they are able. Feelings of sympathy are natural, but moves to take advantage of this wealth of talent in businesses where it is desperately needed, but perhaps not realised, are not as widespread as they should be.

These people can, however, often fill an age gap between those retiring within the next few years and the younger people coming up the ladder. Their experience is of great value if it can be effectively used, if only on a part-time basis. The situation can be utilised by managers who feel that they want to correct the age balance and opportunities to recruit employees in this age group, who have been displaced, are excellent. There are signs in many businesses, deprived of the maturity, sincerity and capacity for dedicated work contained in such people, that they have not been compensated by the bright ideas, enthusiasm and energy of younger people and that the combination of the attributes of both groups has been sadly missed. The so-called 'whizz kid' period is passing into the history of management and there is evidence that employers are again valuing maturity and experience as desirable ingredients of their businesses. Managers who can identify the place of these older people in their departments, fit them into a team containing a wide spread of ages, and lead the team, will be well off for bright ideas and enthusiasm guided and controlled (but not blanketed) by maturity and experience – a priceless combination.

Special induction courses will be needed for this type of person, because of the large amount of previous working experience, probably in a different kind of business. The readjustment element will need special attention to build up confidence and self-respect, and to motivate the new person to the job, the firm and the business. There will be a strong element of fear of the unknown which will have to be dissipated and a tolerant, but not patronising, attitude will make all the difference between success and failure. Special problems may arise in retraining a person to be in contact with the public where experience has been predominantly with things. The example of a craftsman from engineering who becomes a milk roundsman is a good one, where contact with housewives and responsibility for money will be experienced for the first time.

This is a particularly interesting aspect of induction courses and, regrettably, many managers have regarded this type of change as too difficult and have continued the search for scarce younger people who will be looking for more money and will move on without compunction when a more highly paid job comes along. The gratitude felt by older people retrained in the ways described will produce a loyalty and dedication not understood by many younger people with more opportunities, more confidence and fewer disappointments behind him.

There can be no doubt that a professional approach to induction of new employees, no matter what the age or background, must be developed. Getting the right person in the right job has no hope of success without a proper introduction to it under qualified supervision and efficient control. The by-products, such as identification of training needs and personal appraisal, are self-evident and the line manager cannot delay organising his thoughts and actions on the induction of new employees.

8 Promotion and Development

The success of logical and systematic procedures for finding, placing and introducing people to clearly defined and understood jobs depends upon the presence of promotion or development. Development does not necessarily imply promotion and, in many circumstances, two different operations will be involved.

It has been claimed that the days when a person joined a firm to do a job and stayed with that firm until retirement are gone, and there is much truth in this. Most firms, however, still need a solid, reliable, hard core of ordinary people happy to do ordinary jobs. But nowadays there must also be the flexibility and opportunity for those who are worthy, and desirous, to be developed or promoted. If development is not possible in a firm, they should not try to stifle the desire for it if they cannot make use of it. The irresponsible hoarding of stifled and underutilised talent will never help the country's success and it may well be a strong contributor to its failure.

The growth of the interest in manpower planning has been helped by an acceptance of the need to try to plan for the retention of developed people rather than be resigned to losing them. The considerations of promotion and development, and associated techniques, which form part of man-

96

power planning, have regrettably spread only marginally, mostly to the big businesses, but there is an equally great, probably greater, need for them in the smaller firms. The loss of investment in people by smaller firms, which have lost their developed employees to other firms, has prejudiced them against the ideas of manpower planning as a normal management activity. This is understood by the exponents of manpower planning, who tend to rank it with the setting of objectives and motivation of people, and see it as a usual rather than exceptionally difficult activity. This feeling of despair is justified by the attitudes of many line managers who feel that manpower planning is not for them, that it is just too difficult for all kinds of apparently good reasons. They have often not given the matter sufficient, if any, serious thought.

NEED FOR MANPOWER PLANNING

The objective of manpower planning is to have the right people, properly trained and motivated, available for the right jobs when they are available. It is a contributor to the return upon investment outlook which is being encouraged in relation to human resources. There is a very important cost-incentive element to manpower planning, but without adequate attention to all the elements being identified by planning, manpower planning will be a waste of money as it will make available too many people of the wrong kind and too few of the right.

Those who regard manpower planning as so much crystal ball gazing will say that this obsession with the future diverts much-needed attention from the present. The let well alone or 'when we need it we will get it' approach is fine in times of excessive supply at a low price in a buyer's market, but this will never be the situation again. Managers who think it will are living in the past and face a serious problem of personal attitude and outlook change.

Corporate planning, of which manpower planning is an ingredient, is still a developing science. Many valuable opportunities of gaining some experience of it have been lost by attempts to plan too far into the future without built-in flexibility, or by the feeling that the external influences are so great and unpredictable that there is no point in attempting it. This unpredictability is a real consideration – for example, an unexpected strike in the power industry can make nonsense of forward plans which are too inflexible. At worst a forward plan is something that may be departed from, but under control and with knowledge of the factors at work and their implications. There should be identification of the key adjustment areas, rather than a guess at them, or a cutback may result which would be unnecessary if the factors were understood in relation to a plan. At best it will indicate the direction, and level, of investment in people to match the best possible forecast of the company's needs. The day-to-day benefits to be derived from fairly straightforward manpower planning can be:

(a) Determination of recruiting needs.
(b) Anticipation of surpluses to be corrected by natural wastage rather than redundancies or dismissals.
(c) Indication of future training needs.
(d) Provision of a basis for management development programmes.
(e) A factor in industrial relations and productivity bargaining.
(f) Monitoring of labour costs.
(g) Indication of staff facilities required, such as offices, furniture, welfare and social services.
(h) Identification of critical or shortage areas where particular skills or experience will be missing. This is especially important in business diversification and introduction of new technologies.

The matching of future likely demands to future likely supply will rely on the aspects of it under discussion being adequately thought out. An understanding of the jobs to be done and a specification of the people needed to do them will be a basic fact of life for manpower planning conscious managers. Whatever the degree of planning that is accepted as a responsibility of management, manpower planning is at the root of it, which means that the development and promotion of people in the future must be on the agenda of any management committee meeting and firmly in the minds of all managers participating.

SPOTTING TALENT

The attempt to spot talent is often made difficult by lack of information. It is surprising how few line managers have a simple but complete file of information about their staff, starting with basic education and detailing any further education acquired either inside or outside company time. The development by training and acquisition of knowledge or skills in the departmental activities should be on record, indicating the standard of proficiency reached and progress made.

The manager who can take an interest in making notes about his staff will be providing information which can be used when the question of talent is under consideration. In larger firms this is part of the personnel service but it is often not fully effective because to be so it must rely on feed-in of information by way of formal appraisals and informal means. The source of the information must be the line manager who is the key figure and a wealth of information about people has disappeared for ever in many companies because the manager is either not aware of this responsibility or cannot be bothered with it. As a factor in getting the best out of people this wastage of information is almost as serious as the wastage of the people themselves. This may seem an elementary point but it is one that many businesses neglect.

DEVELOPMENT THROUGH PLANNED EXPERIENCE

This expression implies the deliberate provision of different experiences designed to add to the development of the individual in his working environment. As a feature of planned management development programmes it has its advocates and its opponents, but the manager who wishes to satisfy himself that any future candidates for managerial appointments, especially his own successor can carry more load by making them do so, will be in favour of it.

Although management techniques can be taught and discussed, the *ability* to manage can only be tested by providing the opportunity to do so in a situation where the results can be measured. At a senior level, directors of a business who are interested in the availability of departmental and general management talent will wish to see it perform in different situations before being satisfied about its calibre. Many directors like to have young future managers working alongside them on special projects in problem-solving situations and decision-making circumstances before they can be convinced of their suitability. Present managers, who have a more immediate contribution to the total management, may find themselves under scrutiny this way.

The personal assistant approach has been criticised in recent years as not giving genuine responsibility. Assisting with is not the same as carrying responsibility, and is the reason for this criticism. Whilst it is true, nevertheless, the approach by using special projects can achieve two objectives at the same time:

- Defining the project and attaching terms of reference to it which include responsibility for conducting it and selling its conclusion to other managers.
- Facilitating a relationship between the director concerned and the future manager, such that the latter can have his ideas, approaches and style revealed to the director.

The success of any planned experience approach in a management development programme will be dependent upon timing and assurance that the experience really does exist. There will be power to resist diversion from it in face of day-to-day pressures upon apparently higher priority matters and means of validating it – did it achieve what it set out to achieve? Those involved will often find that the desired experience is just not available at the right time anywhere within the company and this is a stumbling block, especially in smaller firms. Co-operation between branches of a firm, geographically separated, for interchange of those under development is not out of the question and represents a source of opportunities for planned experience. This arrangement between firms may be treated with suspicion initially, but there should be enough personal contact between the directors of such firms, especially firms which value business with each other, to make this unwarranted. Interchange of student engineers has benefited from this, for example, often helped by the universities and colleges involved in sandwich courses and appropriate industrial training boards.

There is no reason why this exchange of staff should not be extended to management training and other types of technical training. In the United Kingdom, some training boards have made a big contribution to this aspect of training by helping firms without facilities themselves get their staff into another firm, on an exchange basis. Line managers will need to have this in mind and perhaps develop their own relationships with line managers in other companies, or other branches of their own company.

SELF-DEVELOPMENT

While managers may plan promotion and development for their staff, it is reasonable to expect staff to have ideas for themselves and create opportunities for their own development. This does not always imply extensive study outside working hours and the passing of examinations, although these are to be encouraged when relevant courses are available in the locality. It does imply a willingness to look beyond the day-to-day requirements of the job description, and any person who lets a job build rigid boundaries around him is not looking for development, unless he is under a genuine misunderstanding about it.

There will always be the need for and there will always be staff who are happy within the confines of their job description boundaries, but equally evidence will always be available to the manager who cares to notice it of people who are looking outwards in a positive and sensible way. Staff who are highly motivated by money will be seeking opportunities to earn more and will be interested in development only if this requirement is satisfied. Staff who are motivated by challenge and growth will be looking round for opportunities to add these things to their daily lives.

It is essential for people to take an interest in themselves and make it clear to their managers that they are in the market for development. Exhibition of willingness to tackle special, unusual or unexpected tasks and to rally round in an emergency are clear demonstrations of ambition denied to no one in any working situation. The manager who is noting special information about people will not confine his interest to formal matters but will be adding evidence of desire for self-development whenever he sees it revealed. He will be methodical in noting these matters on his records and will not rely upon his fallible memory. In getting to know people thoroughly the ability to note small, but definite, aspects of behaviour, personality or expertise is part of the skill of management. Day-to-day pressures often push this into the background, but very often the evidence is not available a second time and once it has gone, like time, it has gone for ever.

The welfare state complex has created an expectation of provision for all requirements at all times. In many important areas this is desirable and in cases of misfortune in accidents, health or unemployment it is appropriate that the state system should be available. In matters of self-development the opportunity to be different is there and management is entitled to expect that those who are interested will take advantage of it. This is, however, part of the evidence and cannot be resorted to as a method of providing all the evidence. In some busy situations it is genuinely difficult for those who wish to demonstrate self-development to do so, and this can be very frustrating, leading to resignations and loss of valuable staff in whom an investment has already been made.

USE OF EXTERNAL COURSES

Reference has been made, in Chapter 3, to industry's views upon the need for business schools, and similar considerations apply to external courses relevant to development and promotion needs. The growth of courses since the early

1960s has been tremendous and selecting the appropriate ones has become a difficult problem, especially for the line manager confronted by mountains of literature from all quarters and very little help by way of appraisal of such courses. The first thing the manager needs to be absolutely clear about is the need for, or the reasons for investing money in, releasing a busy person from the staff to attend an external course. It is, however, possible to be fairly specific about this and the following reasons, either singly or in combination, would be usual:

(a) To be taken away from the working environment to mix with people in a similar position and, as a result, modify points of view, widen outlook and be capable of looking at problems differently.
(b) To be detached from working responsibility to concentrate on, and become immersed in, the subject matter of the course followed by the opportunity to think, question and receive guidance.
(c) To hear about the latest ideas on management techniques and practices from experts, have the opportunity to question these and hear other people's reactions to them.
(d) To be introduced to management literature and cultivate the habit of reading. Written work in relation to the literature, by way of analysis, or comment would perhaps follow.
(e) To raise the level of thinking, reading and conversation about serious matters and to have the critical faculty revived.
(f) To receive a strong dose of fresh air.

This can be a formidable experience for a person who is not accustomed to, or who has lost the habit of, this type of activity. Preparatory work before attendance is frequently either not appreciated or neglected, with the result that the person makes a very slow start on the course. There could be barriers of misunderstanding or even fear which should be removed in advance. Ideally the person should be identifying the reasons for attendance, preparing attitudes before going and be happy about the selection of the course. Preparation of domestic affairs should not be neglected if it is a long course, (to some families one week will be a long course). A person who is worried about home and family will not gain maximum advantage because of inadequate attention. Similarly, work load should be catered for or the mind will still be back on the job.

Settling back into the firm, often called the re-entry problem, is equally important, as the benefits of the experience will be lost if the climate upon return is not right for application of the course teaching. In allocating an employee to an external course the manager must accept, and in fact expect, that things will never be the same again if the course has been successful. Armed with increased knowledge, a wider outlook and different attitudes the person concerned will want to do things differently and will press for change. Managers who are unprepared for, or resistant to this must not be surprised if discontent, even conflict arises and, in extreme cases, should help an employee to move elsewhere to circumstances in which the benefits of the training will be more appreciated and utilised.

Managers who are being logical about this aspect of developing staff will want to know about the course programme and objectives. They should find the time to visit the establishment where the course will be held, see the facilities and meet those running it before deciding to use it, and they should also try to make a second visit when the employee is in attendence. Some course organisers provide day appreciation courses to explain their ideas and approaches to managers contemplating their courses. This is an excellent idea, although there is an element of salesmanship. External course relationships should not be developed without approval of the objectives. They can do much harm if approached casually, especially in smaller firms, which generally ought to make much more use of external courses than they do.

PROCEDURE FOR PROMOTION AND DEVELOPMENT ACTIVITIES

Now these general principles have been considered it will be appropriate to outline the approach to implementing them. Line managers will find it useful to be systematic and have stages in mind to develop their thinking and planning of this difficult activity.

IDENTIFY THE NEED FOR SPOTTING TALENT AND DEVELOPING IT

This is a combined thinking and planning process distinguishing between the present and the future on a time scale of perhaps three or four years. On the basis of this thinking and planning, it will have to be accepted that some decisions will turn out to have been wrong as time goes by. The discipline associated with this is similar to that used in general planning and compiling budgets, providing an opportunity to match people to anticipated situations. There will always be a dearth of exact information and facts, and a good deal of judgement will be needed. The desire to develop people must be matched by a desire to make positive plans for the future in spite of information difficulties. Short-term plans are free from this difficulty and experience gained will be valuable in tackling the future possibilities of talent spotting.

COLLECT INFORMATION ABOUT PEOPLE

This needs both personal and departmental records. Plans must relate to the organisation chart. If such a document does not exist the exercise of constructing one will reveal situations previously hidden and will provide a factual reference in identifying needs. The essential information will be concerned with:

- Age structure and impending retirements indicating missing people needed either immediately to balance the age structure, or in the longer term to replace those retiring.
- Lines of communication and chains of command not clear, people reporting to more than one section head, people reporting to no section head at all with lack of controlled delegation.
- People overlapping in certain areas; others in a state of

neglect. Qualification anomalies, underutilisation of them, inappropriate use of them, neglect of them.
- Overstaffing in some sections understaffing in others – staff costs out of line with the output or importance of the section.
- Relevance of the organisation in relation to recent changes, wrong grouping of activities, need for grouping of others.

The departmental organisation chart, kept up to date, is a mine of information and should be part of the wall decoration of any manager's office. This essential starting point for control is, surprisingly, absent from many managers' equipment. There must be an organisation chart for a variety of purposes, but it is imperative in relation to developing and promoting people.

THE ORGANISATION'S SUITABILITY FOR PROMOTION AND DEVELOPMENT

If the manager requires evidence of ability or suitability, the structure of the department, and the company, must be such that there are opportunities built in for this to be possible. Where there is a development programme, positions, sometimes known as staging posts, have to be provided so that employees can train for and do a different job to demonstrate their capabilities. If a section head is moved into responsibility for the work of a different section, it will be necessary for him or her to manage by using the skill and knowledge of the new staff rather than by knowing how to do all the jobs personally. The jacket-off type of supervisor will find this a very challenging situation and their effectiveness will be interesting to observe. Detailed familiarity with the work of a section often produces a 'set in the ways' person who is difficult to develop. Outlooks such as 'If you want a job done properly do it yourself' and 'I would not ask any of my people to do something I cannot do myself' have to be changed if a supervisor is to be developed. Persons who believe these statements have probably reached their ceiling and are not normally suitable for the sort of programmes the manager will be considering.

If this staging post idea is impossible in the organisation

as it is then, before development programmes can be considered, an organisational investigation, followed by changes, will be the first priority. Line managers who have tried to develop people in organisations not suitable for this concept have been severely handicapped, or disillusioned, to the detriment of talent spotting in their departments. The implications of this desire are far-reaching and may influence the entire organisation of the company.

DESIGN OF PERSONAL PROGRAMMES

There can be no standard approach to programmes, although there may be common elements. If it is accepted that all people are individuals and are different, then their development needs and their development programmes will need to be different too. The personal knowledge which the manager has, both on paper and in the mind, will be supplemented by information from the induction course, the basic on-the-job training course, performance on the job, attitudes and personality as revealed by the working environment. Once again this is a matching process, relating knowledge of future job requirements, after promotion, to a knowledge of the person's likely deficiencies. Job descriptions will have to be projected into the future to take account of both internal and external progress. Changes in company products following diversification, changes in technology and political developments, such as entry into the European Economic Community, have recognisable effects, but the forward planning problem will again be present.

Personal development needs will be catered for by a mixture, but an organised mixture, of planned experience, in-company training and attendance at external courses. Responsibility for the detailed plans and supervision of the total course will have to be allocated or looked after by the manager personally. In-company planned experience will depend upon the relationship between the manager concerned and the managers of other departments, as they will be drawing upon one another's facilities if the experience required is not available within the same department. In large companies employing a management development manager, matters of this kind will be organised by this specialist and will depend upon a high-level organisation using the facilities of all departments and all units of the company, including any overseas.

Overseas staging posts are particularly valuable for the development of people, as those involved have to stand on their own feet to a much greater extent when they are deprived of the facilities at home for relying on other people. It is also a highly exciting experience which can be expected to motivate those participating. Through it they are provided with a golden opportunity to show their capabilities.

The programme must be committed to paper and time scales allocated with indication of objectives, course content and means of checking that it has been satisfactorily completed. The person concerned should be a party to its design and dedicated to its implementation.

THE PROMOTION

The total preparatory activity will have succeeded in the short term when promotion follows development and in the long term when the job has been done successfully for a reasonable period of time. Those concerned will then be in a position to start taking an interest in the development of their people as their managers took an interest in developing them, with the added advantage of recent personal experience to draw upon. Having been 'through the mill' they will be well placed to avoid the pitfalls and take advantage of the successes. If they are practising what has been preached they will be concerned about staff resources, gaining knowledge of their value and looking for return upon investment in them. The spread of more enlightened attitudes to promotion and development within an organisation for the first time will depend upon the experiences of those passing through the programmes and setting the pace, perhaps for the first time, in a company.

Experience is accumulating, and so is the literature, by way of case studies from real situations. There is a continuing need for the benefit of experience to be passed along to the new generation of development-minded line managers and they should be prepared to contribute to it themselves.

The relationship between complete company planning,

manpower planning, promotion and development of people is a very close one. Adding an awareness and appreciation of the cost and value of such activities produces a new aspect of business technology. In some organisations management accountancy is being used to embrace these aspects and the scope for down-to-earth management accountants, concerned about value as distinct from cost, is tremendous. Managers themselves must always be prime movers in questions of value, and they must be prepared to utilise their own time better, spending more upon management business than day-to-day routine matters.

The art of delegation is still relatively undeveloped in many businesses and managers who feel that they cannot find the time and the inclination to spot talent, organise promotion and development schemes, assess external courses and appraise success or failure in these things are displaying an inability to delegate and casting doubts on their own ability to manage. The development of supervisors and section leaders to pull the day-to-day load is one of the top development priorities today.

9 Appraisal and Rewards

Managers who are concerned about the performance of their employees, after taking care about their selection, placement and training, will be seeking ways of measuring it and will quickly realise how difficult this is. Managers from a technical or marketing background will be accustomed to measuring things, receiving information and statistics against which they can decide how well things are going without much difficulty. The measurement of performance has exercised the minds, and the researches, of many clever people but it is not yet an exact science and probably never will be.

NEED FOR MEASUREMENT

Educationalists have been measuring people for many years by means of examinations and such related activities as essays, theses on the basis of research or projects, and oral and written work. The increased amount of contact between higher educationalists and industrialists, fostered by the growth of sandwich and postgraduate courses, has developed educationalists' interest in the possibility of examining people in industry, or at the place of work, as well as at college or university. The assessment of industrial training as part of a sandwich course, for instance, has caused much head scratching as, in such a course, it is theoretically possible to fail because of inadequate or unsatisfactory industrial training. It is an out-of-balance arrangement, however, as failure to pass the college examinations is obvious from the marks gained in them whereas failure to pass the training cannot be indicated in such a straight-forward way.

Personal factors such as attitude, temperament, qualities of leadership, etc. have become more important as more open, and less dictatorial, styles of management have spread. Consequently the need to measure the abstract or intangible factors of people has grown. The personality tests referred to in Chapter 5 are relevant just as much in appraisal of performance as they are in original selection. Many line managers feel that tests of this kind are academic but they are worthy of serious thought and a change in managerial outlook about them must be made. As explained in Chapter 5, however, they are not for the amateur, and specialist help in the introduction of personality or tempera-ment tests is advisable.

PERFORMANCE APPRAISAL IN THE PAST

Many managers will be familiar with forms used in the past either in assessment of themselves or other people. These forms have relied upon the personal judgement of those involved and the designers of such forms have indicated the need to be interested in matters such as:

- Punctuality
- Personality
- Co-operativeness
- Ability to get on with people
- Willingness
- Conscientiousness
- Capacity for hard work
- Ability to get things done

All very serious matters covering qualities of great value to the manager in running his department. But how can such things be measured? By judgement only, and personal judgement is notorious for its fallibility, especially when one human being is judged by another. This is not a new discovery yet it is extraordinary that so many managers have still advanced no further than the assessment of these qualities by personal judgement. It is worrying that rating of performance continues to be highly subjective.

With business under increasing pressure, managers must be constantly concerned with the efficient utilisation of all their resources. When so much is known about the utilisation of money, materials and machinery it is unacceptable to use only subjective methods when dealing with the utilisation of people. Appraisal of people is a high-priority matter, a specific responsibility of management, something to be applied to everybody, including the manager himself. The past history of appraisals indicates that they have given all kinds of interesting information but have rarely answered the question 'How well is the person doing at the job he has been paid to do?' This is our starting point.

IS APPRAISAL POSSIBLE?

Appraisal is part of a complete approach to getting the best out of people by being aware of, and putting into practice, the ideas in this book. Any manager who feels that one must go for appraisal right away will quickly appreciate the difficulties and will go back to the beginning of this chapter, appreciating that measurement is desirable but that there is no ready method available. The desire to create one will focus attention back to other subjects like job descriptions, setting of targets and objectives.

The complete company situation is the point to begin from. In businesses where developments such as work study, identification of training needs, review of payment and bonus system related to some form of measurement, surveys by management consultants and introduction of manage-ment committees have recently taken place, there will be, at least, thinking and receptiveness to change; at most, information which can be used as a basis for measurements.

To start from scratch, where the general management is unreceptive to the notion, would be a formidable challenge.

There are many examples of attempts to introduce appraisal schemes which have repeated mistakes made by others. Attempts to copy a success in one firm can be unsuccessful in another firm because of fundamental differences between them. It is most unlikely that a well thought-out scheme used in one firm can be translated without modification to another firm. The principles of approach and lessons learnt can certainly be valuable, but staff and job differences may be considerable. Managers will, therefore, be anxious to draw upon other people's ideas and experience, but, as with most things in business life, they will have to create their own details if the appraisal scheme is to match the requirement. They should be interested in the principle of designing appraisal schemes, not looking for a ready-made package which can be applied and left to run itself.

PRINCIPLES OF APPRAISAL SCHEMES

The following questions will have to be considered:

WHAT IS THE NEED FOR APPRAISAL?

Usually to indicate effectiveness in the day-to-day job, leading to identification of satisfactory and unsatisfactory aspect of performance. Strengths can then be developed and weaknesses rectified so far as is possible. This will also reveal misfits from opposing points of view – too good and not good enough.

WILL IT BE REQUIRED TO INDICATE TRAINING NEEDS?

Most likely this will be so and if appraisal is identifying areas of weakness the implication will be either bad selection by putting the wrong person in the job in the first place or inadequate training. Obsolescence may be the problem, especially in a manager, and the opportunity to assess the ability to keep up to date will be built into an appraisal.

WILL IT HELP AS A TALENT SPOTTER?

To avoid the temptation to try to do too much in a scheme

the purpose of the appraisal needs to be clear. It will probably not be sensible to try to do everything at the same time, as confusion is bound to arise and the fringe aspect will detract from its main purpose. If the main purpose is to indicate success in the present job it may not be appropriate to try to measure potential at the same time, as the job may not itself be suitable as an indicator of potential. However, this may be possible and reasonable in relation to some jobs.

WILL A STANDARD SCHEME BE SUITABLE FOR ALL LEVELS IN THE DEPARTMENT?

If this can be managed then there is a great saving in complication. However, it is reasonable to expect that the manager will be looking for a different kind of contribution from a section leader to that from a filing clerk, and, while it will be of equal importance to appraise how they are both performing, it is likely that the factors of importance and identification of needs will be so different that a diversity approach will probably be imperative.

HOW OFTEN WILL APPRAISAL BE NECESSARY AND WILL THE SAME FREQUENCY BE NEEDED FOR ALL LEVELS?

For junior staff, appraisal related to a birthday salary reveiw, on a wage-for-age basis, is a well-established ritual that is recognised as an opportunity to review the situation, mainly from a judgement point of view. To perpetuate rituals of this kind cannot be regarded as acceptable practice and any wage-for-age system has nothing to commend it, except simplicity. Things that are regular do have a ritual flavour about them but the good appraisal scheme will be related to job factors, not time factors.

The question of when and how often is difficult to answer and striking a balance between making it a ritual and doing it when the need arises is a difficult one. Many schemes are attached to salary review, either yearly or half yearly, and there is a strong feeling that appraisal of performance, while it influences salary changes, should be separated from talks about money. Others take the opposite view, saying that performance and salary increases are the same thing so they should be bracketed together – performance leads to salary change. Individual managers will have to work this one out for themselves as they feel appropriate in their own scheme of management. The important thing is that whatever the outlook on this matter of appraisal, opportunities to learn about people from both the good and bad things they do should be taken advantage of.

There will always be special situations, as in the case of a manager developing a successor to a person retiring in the near future. Appraisal of several people against carefully planned changes in their responsibilities may be needed at short intervals of, say, a month as an aid to making the decision on which is the right person for the promotion. The relationship between planned development and performance appraisal is a close one and managers who know what they are looking for will be well placed to design an appraisal procedure for themselves, or be specific to the personnel manager, if providing the service. When depends upon why, which follows how.

IS IT A GOOD IDEA TO CONSULT THOSE WHO ARE TO BE APPRAISED ABOUT HOW THEY SHOULD BE APPRAISED?

The value of the quiet and unobtrusive, possibly secretive, approach to appraisal is questionable. The enlightened manager, who is interested in human relationships, will wish to involve those affected in thoughts about measuring their performance. Looking ahead to the time when the results of an appraisal will be challenged and decisions based upon it justified or defended, managers will wish to protect their position and be confident that the scheme will stand up to this test. It must be expected that appraisals, especially when they lead to unpleasant or delicate decisions, will be challenged and those concerned have a right to know what is the basis of, or evidence to support, such decisions. Impositions will tend to be resisted and they will provoke conflict if they are not understood and accepted.

The spread of collective bargaining and representation in white-collar situations makes it inevitable that procedures affecting the jobs, lives and earnings of people will be challenged not only by individuals but by groups destined to become much more powerful. It is not suggested that the manager should abdicate from such procedures as being too difficult and controversial, as the need for them is likely to increase. It is suggested the reasons will have to be clear and the people involved will have to be consulted, or at least given adequate acceptable explanation, when new methods of appraising them are being contemplated. They must be taken seriously not only by those doing the appraising but by those being appraised, and a silent revolt will sabotage any attempts to impose such an appraisal. Consultation, from a strong and properly thought-out management position, is required in spreading the use, and value, to both sides of new or improved appraisal schemes, backed by sound reasons and principles of approach capable of standing up to challenge and examination. Secrecy will eliminate immediately any prospects of acceptance and ultimate success.

INTRODUCTION AND EXPLANATION OF THE SCHEME

This is an internal communication exercise which cannot be delegated. To explain formally the reasons for, and method of, operation will be essential before an appraisal scheme is introduced. From time to time it will also be necessary to inform about progress and success of the scheme, what benefits have been derived from it and what is its value to the firm, the department and the individual.

PREPARATION OF SUPERVISORS TO APPRAISE THEIR OWN STAFF

Although the need for and creation of the scheme cannot be delegated, the manager can and must delegate its operation to those managing others, irrespective of level. This produces a training requirement for these supervisors in the operation and mechanics of appraisal, and, more than likely, for managers themselves. Where numbers justify it, a specially designed in-company training course will be appropriate, run by either the personnel manager or an external organisation. The course will first inform about the scheme then give experience in its operation under controlled and qualified tuition or guidance. Since interviewing will usually form one of the stages of an appraisal activity the subjects of interviewing and assessing reactions will be equally important. There may be an overlap here with courses on recruiting methods and an appropriate in-company course for supervisors may well cover both matters simultaneously so that they receive training in both selection and appraisal in one specially designed course.

Supervisors and managers attending external courses will be exposed to ideas about appraisal for various purposes and will be able to apply these lessons when they return. Experience from different types of business is of value and the benefit of experience, and lessons learnt from it, can be discussed on such courses. An individual scheme for each firm will usually be needed, followed by special training in its operation. Training arrangements for those involved will not only enable them to make a better job of it but will give status and seriousness to it – which it must have if a 'playing about with it' feeling is to be dissipated. It must be adequately thought out and prepared, be conducted by properly trained, dedicated people who are clear about its aims and objectives.

PLACING ONESELF IN THE SHOES OF THOSE BEING APPRAISED

This will anticipate some of the reactions, misgivings and suspicions about it. To attempt to appraise people in a job where there is no job description, to compare them with targets or objectives when they are not known or not accepted as reasonable or achievable because of factors outside personal control, is clearly nonsense. Managers have been known to make attempts under these circumstances with predictable results. If people have made constructive and sensible proposals for improving the efficiency of their work or its effectiveness in relation to the whole work which have either been ignored, or rejected, for unsound reasons, it is unlikely that they will be receptive to appraisal until things have either been put right or sound acceptable reasons given for rejecting their ideas. Managers must be prepared to consider reactions of this kind and cope with them before they advance too far with appraisal plans.

While schemes may be first rate, there may be substantial barriers to acceptance which they will have to demolish before they can move forward.

INFORMAL APPRAISAL

In general it is understood that managers are informally assessing their people all the time, but not in a systematic or objective way. The point is not that this informal assessment should be replaced by the measurement ideas in an appraisal scheme – the two are needed. The manager who is alert to the need for appraisal of any kind, will take advantage of every contact opportunity to get to know people better, and will even take note of dropped hints, whether deliberate or not, in the task of getting the right people in the right jobs. Information usually comes not to order but when least expected, when the manager is least prepared for it. The combination of the informal 'getting to know you' approach and formal appraisal in a measured way must be maintained. Traditional so-called appraisals based upon subjective judgement must be replaced by something independent of personal like or dislike, more related to ability to do the job. A checklist approach, based on the points discussed, should enable managers to work out their own principles of approach and not forget important down-to-earth aspects of their own individual working situation.

RELATIONSHIP BETWEEN MANAGEMENT BY OBJECTIVES AND APPRAISAL OF STAFF

Consideration of the subject of management by objectives will cover the same ground as that covered by appraisal schemes. They are both concerned with job, or situation, measurements and the replacement of opinion and judgement by quantifiable facts. Managers familiar with the management by objectives concept will know that it is dependent upon the following:

(a) Telling people clearly and specifically what they are required to do, providing them with the resources,

organisation and environment in which they can discuss the desired results.
(b) Knowledge of the company's overall performance and achievement plans into which departmental objectives can be placed.
(c) Clarity about, and acceptance of, the key results and performance standards to be achieved consistent with these company plans.
(d) Organisation and control supported by flexibility to operate in key result areas.
(e) Performance review and potential review to identify, measure and analyse progress in relation to plans.
(f) Development and motivation of managers with opportunities for training to help overcome weaknesses and bring out strengths.

John Humble, discussing management development in relation to management by objectives, suggests that managers have five basic needs which must be satisfied if they are to meet the objectives contained in the key result areas. They are as follows:

- Agree with me the results I am to achieve.
- Give me an opportunity to perform.
- Let me know how I am getting on.
- Give me guidance and training.
- Reward and promote me on my contribution.

The interrelationship between setting objectives, appraisal of performance and rewards is clearly established in these statements. In appraisal situations the availability of knowledge about the key result areas, the achievements they must contain, and something to measure, gives managers a starting point in the design of their schemes. When people are doing well it is easy for appraisers to hand out compliments, as this is a pleasant thing to do whether there are clear key areas or not. In the reverse situation the prospect of telling people they have done badly is never looked forward to by a manager and the key areas will provide the evidence needed to give a basis for discussion with some confidence. The distinction between performance review, potential review and salary review can be looked upon as showing what has been achieved, what must happen next and what has it all been worth. The objectives approach distinguishes the differences and avoids the confusion discussed earlier.

Departmental objectives are calculated in relation to company objectives, although absence of the latter does not excuse neglect of the former. If appraisal is going to be based upon something which can be measured then the setting of departmental objectives must be tackled first. The difficulty of quantifying the tasks of some departments should not be underestimated; nor can the ability of management to think of output in these terms be developed overnight. If company attitudes are unreceptive to objectives, individual managers will be thrown upon their own dedication to, and enthusiasm for, managing their own departments in this way, even if the company is not. In practice there are very few situations which cannot have objectives attached to them and appraisal schemes will be directly related to these.

The point made previously, that objectives cannot be imposed but must be discussed, developed and agreed with those responsible for meeting them, must be emphasised again. Departmental thinking about such matters may be the forerunner of company thinking and the forward-looking manager will be setting the pace for the others. The discipline attached to identifying objectives and relating performance to them is worthwhile in itself as it provides the opportunity to go back to first principles and ask fundamental questions about the work and reasons for it. Appraisal by measurement is a component of the management style based on information, it cannot be added to outdated styles based on judgement and opinion. Management by objectives is also very much a part of this and its relevance to appraisal is established.

SALARY APPRAISAL

Though it can be understood, for purposes of simplicity, that assessment of worth as indicated by financial rewards could be a separate activity, the findings of performance appraisal will provide the information upon which decisions about worth will be made. To establish outstanding performance and then to improve rewards only marginally is clearly nonsense. If the approach to performance appraisal is going to be objective, so must be the approach to rewards. Of course money is not always the chief motivator, but attempts to motivate by interest and job satisfaction will get nowhere if the approach to rewards is such as to produce dissatisfaction.

Attention to the financial rewards package is, therefore, part of the complete examination of performance. Packages have become more varied in recent years because of high taxation, especially at managerial level, and attempts to increase rewards within the taxation laws have produced interesting possibilities. In fact an important factor in fixing a salary is often to consider the value of the fringe benefits first rather than last. The skill required to compile the package is not negligible and there is much scope for managers to increase the rewards of their jobs without increasing taxable salary and without breaking the law. Because of the legal aspect, payment packages have produced a growth area of business for insurance companies and chartered accountants either offering or scrutinising schemes often based upon insurance approaches, especially life assurance.

In some appointments there is no confusion about salary payments because the payment is related to some kind of scale, irrespective of success or failure. It usually continues for normal periods of sickness, accident, holidays or other approved absences without question, giving a security element to the system. Bonus or profit-sharing schemes for non-productive or service staff, based on the performance of directly productive workers, are fairly common, so that some financial benefit from the company's prosperity can be passed on to those unable to influence it directly, but having a marked influence upon it indirectly.

In directly productive jobs, however, the tradition has been to link rewards to output but such schemes are now being modified to include more security, catering for sickness and holidays and related to productive time. It is sensible to relate higher rewards to higher output and better performance and productivity agreements designed to guarantee additional financial benefits for guaranteed higher output have been reached in many industries.

Experience with work measurement, method study and skills analysis has identified the important ingredients of productive jobs (analogous to key task areas for managers) leading to job descriptions for trades or skills commonly to be found in certain industries. In such cases, individual appraisal is a non-starter because of the numbers involved and instead a system known as job evaluation has been used. There is much literature about how job evaluation based upon a comparison of job skill, knowledge and experience with special factors, such as unpleasant working conditions, produces job gradings or ratings in categories. Scales or bands of payment can be added to the gradings with bonus or profit-sharing elements. Introduction of job evaluation, which can apply equally well to offices, puts a responsibility upon supervision to keep the unit fully occupied, because payment is not directly dependent upon output and management or organisational delays will introduce inefficiency, followed by excessive costs.

As with performance appraisal there is a continual search for salary appraisal systems based upon measurements rather than tradition or keeping up with market prices. It is interesting to note that this approach, which has so much to commend it, has been used on only a limited scale in productive situations, and hardly at all in offices. The impact of inflation creates confusion between increases to maintain position in relation to the national cost of living and increases for merit. Regrettably many people are finding merit placed second as employers struggle to keep up with cost-of-living increases. Those who deserve much to reward personal merit tend to fall behind and lose their differential in relation to the average.

The fringe benefit possibilities must also be kept in mind as they can do much to compensate for this difficulty. The most usual are non-contributory pension and life insurance schemes, provision of a company car and subsidised meals. For executives, share purchase schemes and membership of private health care schemes are growing in popularity.

Subsidised or special rate mortgages are usual in banks and financial businesses.

The manager's approach to the introduction of new payments systems, such as job evaluation, incentive schemes or productivity agreements supporting increased earning power, will need the same level of communication as for appraisal schemes. They cannot be imposed but must be explained, discussed and negotiated about before they can be introduced. Again employee representation will be powerful and in money matters of this kind management must take the initiative with unions, not wait for them to react. Continual monitoring is essential, with flexibility to make changes possible when the objectives are not being achieved or when unforeseen snags arise. This must be the manager's outlook on assessing and rewarding people, based on sound principles relevant to the particular part of the business and staff manager is responsible for.

REFERENCES

John Humble, *Management by Objectives in Action,* McGraw-Hill, 1970.
T.T. Patterson, *Job Evaluation,* Business Books.

10 Legislation and Communication

During the last ten years personnel management in the United Kingdom has been the subject of unprecedented attention. Its conservative, low key, fringe role predominantly concerned with record keeping and welfare has been demolished and will never be seen again. From a position on the periphery of line management it is now generally accepted as an integral part of the line management process and the personnel director is no longer quite so conspicuously absent from the board room as was the case ten years ago.

Not only in management, but in the trade unions, the passing of the old brigade into retirement has brought new types of leader to the fore. Union officials with higher education, and the benefit of the thorough training for which the trade union business is well known, found it easy to gain the upper hand over management, especially at supervisory level, and they began to set the pace.

Rumblings about bringing human working relationships within the framework of the law culminated in the passing of the Industrial Relations Act introduced in 1971 by the Conservative government. However, the provisions of the Act were given little opportunity to operate. The change of government provided a good opportunity to think again and in 1975 the Labour government repealed the 1971 Act and replaced it with the Trade Union and Labour Relations Act 1974 which was followed by the Employment Protection Act 1975. Other important legislation was concerned with equal pay, equal work, sex discrimination, and health and safety at work. It is not the intention to deal with the details of this legislation here since it has been adequately covered in numerous publications. It is also not of direct interest to readers outside the United Kingdom who will probably have their own legislation to contend with. However, the principles, and effect, of this legislation will enable experience to be applied in any place where human relationships in the working situation are of concern.

GENERAL PRINCIPLES OF LEGISLATION

The first principle of legislation is that it should not be regarded as a punishment for bad personnel management but as a motivator for better personnel management. There is no doubt, however, that the punishments for not implementing legislation in a company can be severe. There is, equally, no doubt that many companies have not entered into the spirit of it and taken the attitude that it is easier, and cheaper, to suffer punishment if at fault rather than make provision to avoid such punishment. Many managers taking this line have found that:

- It usually costs more in direct compensation payments than anticipated.
- It is expensive to have productive time diverted into dealing with disputes and tribunals which are negative and unproductive.
- The publicity is embarrassing and uncomfortable and leads to unrest and a fall in employee morale.
- The process of conflict can be exhausting.

The second principle of legislation is based upon the belief that prevention is better than cure, which has always been a difficult commodity to sell. The approach to applying this philosophy requires:

(a) A thorough investigation of the company's present practices and procedures of personnel management.
(b) Comparison of these with the requirements of legislation and good, current personnel outlooks.
(c) Clear identification of the person responsible for personnel management and human relationships affairs.
(d) Modification of, and improvement to, the practices and procedures to ensure that prevention is built into them.
(e) Establishment of appropriate practices and procedures where there is an absence of them.
(f) Monitoring and control of these so that there is flexibility and provision for change where necessary.

This is a neglected area of line management and, in companies employing full-time, qualified personnel management staff, line managers will feel this is not one of their problems. Up to a point this is a reasonable view but there cannot be complete delegation of these matters to the personnel department. The division of responsibility is such that personnel staff should be providing the guidance, clerical back-up and unbiased view of the principles to be applied, whereas line managers, who will have to live with and implement the principles, must be party to them. In companies where the employment of full-time personnel staff is not justified help will be needed either from the company secretary or an outside organisation. Help of the latter kind is readily available from organisations such as trade federations, chambers of commerce and management consultants. This matter of organising and managing people in accordance with the rules of the game is an international one although the rules may differ in different countries. To continue the neglect of this aspect of line management will be to continue the growth of the industrial lawyer business and the appeals tribunal business, neither of which can contribute directly to productivity improvement. It can be argued that exposure to these matters will cause lessons to be learned and a dedication to the avoidance of them in the future which can help productivity. Managers who have grown into their managerial positions the hard way will have built into them a learning by mistakes outlook and they will feel that this outlook will work in the application of legislation. Attitude changes are the most difficult of all to make and a critical self-appraisal will be imperative for many such managers if they are to survive themselves.

SOME SPECIFIC PRINCIPLES

Although general reaction to it has been that the introduction of legislation into the management of people is the last straw, it must be conceded that much good has emerged from it. For instance, there can be no doubt that personnel management in the United Kingdom has benefited. Businesses with well-thought-out practices and procedures that agree in general with the legislation regard legislation as an unsolicited testimonial for themselves and they have needed to make changes only in a limited, but nevertheless worthwhile, way. Those companies who have not, or who are resistant to the requirements imposed, must think about the following:

(a) It is a fundamental right, irrespective of the law, that employees at all levels should know precisely what is their job, what terms and conditions apply to it and what are their rights in relation to it. There must be a brief, but adequate, job description document.

(b) A statement of the terms and conditions applicable to the appointment must be given to each employee not later than thirteen weeks after commencing employment. The law requires this in the United Kingdom. This principle is so obvious that legislation should not have been required to apply it. The key contents of this statement are:

> Naming of the employer and the employee.
> The date employment commenced.
> Noting of any previous employment which counts towards continuous service.
> Scale and rate of remuneration – frequency of payment.
> Hours of work, holiday entitlement and sickness arrangement.
> Pension and insurance provisions.

Length of notice of termination of employment.
Job title.
Disciplinary matters.
Grievance procedures.
Safety arrangements and procedures.

(c) Personnel practices and procedures must be reviewed regularly after being correctly established and agreed initially. These cannot be devised and applied unilaterally by line managers but must be the subject of consultation between managers and employees (or their recognised representatives). The procedural framework must suit the company and its style of management first and foremost, then take account of legislation. To impose legislation requirements in a way which is inappropriate for the style of the company will lead to failure in applying this principle.

(d) The procedures, elaboration of terms and conditions plus any other appropriate information not covered by legislation but intended to inform the employees of company outlook, objectives and methods of operation can conveniently be gathered into a company handbook. This is a much neglected principle and line managers should take a look at it. Having produced it many companies allow it to be neglected or fall into disuse but it should be a living document, available to all and up to date.

(e) There must be a senior person in the company with a clearly defined responsibility for personnel matters. If a full-time appointment to this function is not justified, line managers will often have to take the initiative in getting this responsibility allocated to somebody. It is not advocated that the line managers should spend their time devising terms and conditions of employment, and writing company handbooks. It is advocated however that they should convince the owners or directors of their businesses that action is imperative. Frequently it is necessary to engage outside expert assistance to get these matters organised and established after which the company secretary or the financial controller, with clerical assistance, will be able to cope and maintain systems rather than create them.

(f) Because of the well-established unfair dismissal procedure, supported by six years of experience, it must be a principle to take every possible step at all stages of employment to ensure that the company is protected against unfair dismissal situations. Initially line managers felt very threatened by the rules applicable to this aspect of their jobs and a well-established feeling arose that the requirements were so difficult that it would no longer be possible to dismiss anybody. Fortunately this feeling has passed generally but it is essential that the following matters receive attention:

(i) There must be selection methods to ensure that the right people are selected in the first place. Removal of the wrong people is more difficult than getting the selection right in the first place.

(ii) There must be adequate records supporting the terms and conditions of employment so that there is no doubt about such facts as starting date, appraisal interviews, records of performance, absence from work and promotion into areas of greater responsibility.

(iii) There must be a suitable performance appraisal scheme which has been explained and accepted by employees (or their recognised representatives).

(iv) There must be a recognised warnings procedure in cases of unsatisfactory work performance, conduct or attendance. An established procedure in common use in the United Kingdom is to give a verbal warning, followed by two written warnings, which, if unheeded, will lead to dismissal. These warnings must be recorded on the employee's record.

(g) A final specific principle is to implement the material of this book. Whilst legislation has found a permanent place in the personnel and line management functions it is the line manager who has come to terms with the need to get the right person in the right job in a positive working climate, protected by legislation but not managed by it.

EFFECT OF LEGISLATION

In considering the background to, and principles of, personnel legislation it has to be emphasised that, although it has been in existence for ten years in the United Kingdom, there are still too many companies, and line managers within those companies, who have not taken the sensible options open to them. The major result of legislation should be greater productivity through the employment of well-organised, reasonably protected people, in a positive working environment, but the present international recessionary condition suggests that something has gone wrong. The sum total of individual line management inadequacies has contributed to this. There has been some resentment of the effect of legislation in placing too much emphasis upon employee rights and too little upon employee obligations. Line managers feel that their authority has been undermined by this effect. As a consequence a tendency to be passive and let events take their course is evident and the challenge of the 1980s is to change this state of mind to a desire to get this effect under control and see it as a contribution to better management. Line managers will acknowledge that, when they are faced up to and put in perspective, the effects of legislation not only take a number of delicate, discretionary areas out of their hair but also protect the managers themselves as individuals as well as protecting the employees for whom they are responsible.

Certain specific effects of legislation can be selected for more detailed thought:

DISCIPLINE

Line managers who have been in line management for about twenty years, who have been accustomed to a personal style of management based upon knowing all the employees and being on first-name terms with most of them, have generally reacted strongly against spelling out disciplinary rules. Their certainty that everybody knows the disciplinary rules in the department because they are obvious and common sense makes them think it nonsense to put these down on paper as an ingredient of the terms and conditions of employment. Unfair dismissal cases have thrived upon this false certainty and the following example of the approach to specifying these matters will help line managers to adjust their thinking and take action. The sorts of employee misbehaviour likely to result in disciplinary action include:

- Insubordination.
- Poor timekeeping.
- Unauthorised absence.
- Giving false information to excuse absence.
- Misconduct.
- Gambling on the company's premises.
- Irresponsible or offensive behaviour at work.
- Use of abusive language.
- Unacceptable standards of personal appearance.
- Practical joking on the company's premises.
- Smoking in prohibited areas.
- Intoxication on the company's premises.
- Carelessness in relation to the safety policy of the company.
- Engaging in work which is not related to the company's business on company premises, in company time without permission.
- Refusal to carry out a reasonable instruction.
- Failure to meet required performance standards.

It must be acknowledged that these items are, in general, common sense but the interpretation of them cannot be left to common sense. If the example of insubordination is taken then the question is – what constitutes insubordination? The line manager who dismisses an employee on the spot because that was what was done ten years ago is probably in for a shock. An unfair dismissal claim referred to a tribunal will demonstrate fairly rapidly that the manager has acted unreasonably and reinstatement, or compensation, will be ordered. The interpretations of insubordination, refusal to carry out a reasonable instruction and unacceptable standards of appearance are especially difficult. The need for caution is so obvious here that it need not be dwelt upon, but nevertheless there must be control stemming from clarity, of requirement, of instruction and about the consequence of offences.

Examples of employee misbehaviour likely to result in dismissal, without notice, include:
- Theft from the company's premises or employees.
- Fraud (in relation to employment with the company).
- Dishonesty (in relation to employment with the company).
- Breach of the company's security procedure.
- Divulging confidential information without authorisation.
- Providing misleading information at the commencement of employment.
- Physical assault.
- Fighting on the company's premises.
- Committing a serious breach of the company's ethical requirements.
- Engaging on one's own account in any trade, profession or business, either directly or indirectly, as principal or agent, without the company's permission.
- Committing any act likely to bring the company into disrepute.
- Purporting to act on behalf of the company without the required authorisation.
- Deliberate misappropriation of the funds of the company or its clients.
- Wilful damage to the company's property.
- Any criminal offence which is likely to adversely affect employment with the company.
- Any act of gross misconduct not mentioned above.

These are all highly serious matters and extreme caution in dealing with them is vital. Summary dismissal under these headings requires managers with cool heads and clear thinking backed by clear definitions and procedures.

GRIEVANCE AND DISCIPLINARY PROCEDURE

Grievances should be ventilated with the line manager first and foremost to eliminate the possibility of them being submerged or grumbled about in small groups or within a department, or taken initially to the shop steward. Procedure is important here: it must be agreed by the parties concerned, then adhered to. The following of procedure is a well-developed art in trade union circles but not so in line management where informality has prevailed. Nevertheless it must be recognised that the best-developed and understood procedure is sometimes by-passed, when expedient, which does not help to encourage its establishment in line management. It is, however, a fact that the terms of employment legislation require an indication of this procedure for all employees and the document must state, preferably by name, the person to whom grievances should be reported and the further procedure if there is dissatisfaction with the outcome of the discussion. Disciplinary procedure can be illustrated in the following example:

Company policy will observe the following procedural stages:

Stage 1 – Discussion in a relaxed way between the manager and the employee concerned of the grievance or disciplinary problem, followed by a verbal warning if appropriate which must be recorded on the employee's record document.

Stage 2 – If the required improvement is not forthcoming a written warning will be issued after further discussion.

Stage 3 – If there is still the same problem a second written warning will be issued indicating that if the problem is not solved within a certain time dismissal will follow. At this stage it will be prudent for line managers to bring in their own superior.

Stage 4 – Termination of employment.

Every opportunity must be given to an employee in these circumstances to reply to criticism and discuss the reasons for the problem. If it concerns job performance there could be important factors such as inadequate training, lack of equipment or resources or the giving of unclear instructions by the manager. In any disciplinary interview the employee can be accompanied by a friend or a colleague and appeal to a higher level should always be possible, especially where termination of employment is a possibility. In summary dismissal cases suspension on full pay is usual whilst the circumstances are investigated in full and a decision justified. After the passage of one year oral or written warnings should be removed from the record if there has been no repetition of the problem and it can be assumed that it has been solved.

It cannot be overemphasised that in this area of grievance, discipline and procedures the line manager must take the initiative and remain in command of the situation. The expression of dissatisfaction in a working situation can come from any point in a department and is unpredictable, but it generally comes in one or other of two forms. In the first manifest expression of discontent, individual or group, will be there for all to see and can lead eventually to a strike. The second form, latent discontent, will be not so obvious and will be felt as lower morale, drop in output, increases in error, absenteeism and labour turnover. Both forms create management problems and negative attitudes.

EQUAL PAY AND OPPORTUNITIES

Discrimination on grounds of sex or race is illegal in the United Kingdom. Legislation requires equal pay for equal work and equal opportunities of employment. Any intent (or hidden intent) to discriminate will lead to problems and line managers must take particular care in this aspect of their working lives. Starting with job advertisements, job descriptions and employee development there must be an indication that equal opportunities really do exist. To introduce equal pay for men and women, for example, and then to screen women out of certain jobs would clearly create a false situation with attendant problems. The only exceptions where sex is a genuine occupational matter are, for example:

- Modelling or acting.
- Personal privacy – such as lavatory attendants.
- Type of establishment in which the work has to be performed – prison warder.
- Where sleeping on the premises is required and there is no separate accommodation.
- Where safety, health or welfare reasons dominate.
- Where married couples would be inappropriate.

- In overseas countries where the laws or customs would not allow the employment of a woman - such as Nigeria or Saudi Arabia.

Under this heading are maternity arrangements where United Kingdom legislation does not allow discrimination between a husband and wife. That means the mother has equal rights with the father for continuity of employment, although, in the mother's case, it is obvious that a period of absence must be allowed for her to have the baby. The statutory arrangements for maternity pay, preservation of job rights and return to work are clear and should be applied as normal practice. Line managers must be aware of these since the engagement of a replacement for a woman taking maternity leave who wishes to exercise her rights must be carefully handled. The job available to the replacement will be for the period of maternity leave only and the replacement must be officially aware of this.

REDUNDANCY

In recent times managers have become all too familiar with the legislation on redundancy. The rules are now well established in the United Kingdom and the benefits provided have enabled many people, unfortunately forced into unemployment or a career change late in life, to survive. Line managers themselves have been amongst those affected and a realistic, but compassionate, approach has spread. Opportunities to apply for new jobs, career counselling and facilities for training are positive steps which line managers have been able to take as positive supplements to ensuring that financial entitlements are met. Redundancy has brought into prominence the need for correct records to establish length of service in certain age brackets, adequate job descriptions to match employees' ability to transfer from a redundant appointment to an alternative appointment which is vacant.

Whilst redundancy is a real misfortune it is beyond doubt that much of United Kingdom commerce and industry has been overstaffed and that people have been recruited unthinkingly and indiscriminately in ways so often referred to

in this book. Application of the ideas advocated in it may
help to avoid such problems in the future.

COMMUNICATION AND THE LINE MANAGER

Communication is a much over-worked word and there are
those who think we suffer from too much of it. It is
nevertheless appropriate to pass from redundancy as a
legislation matter to redundancy as a communications
matter. Line managers can be forgiven for feeling that there
is too much communication already. Faced as they are with
the day-to-day pressures of survival, they are in no mood to
read at home and they have no hope at all of reading at work.
For it has been made abundantly clear in the past two years
that communication is not only a question of individual or
group face-to-face situations, but of being knowledgeable
about facts and pitfalls in applying facts. The communications business in the United Kingdom took off after the 1975
legislation referred to in this chapter. Terms and conditions,
grievance procedures and disciplinary rules had to be
applied and instances of unfair dismissal cases grew rapidly
in the wake of inadequate personnel systems and, above all,
hopelessly inadequate communication. The recent recession
took large numbers of people completely by surprise as their
jobs disappeared virtually overnight. The surprise and
bewilderment involved have brought into prominence yet
again our old friend communication – or the lack of it.

PARTICIPATION

In recent cutbacks and failures of various businesses there
has been a justified criticism of managers at all levels,
including owners and chairmen. The communication gap
between those who know the facts and those who suffer as a
consequence of them has produced large-scale human
misery which the next generation of line managers will have
to deal with as they attempt to build up businesses once more
and restore the morale of people working in them.
    The subject of participation, which is not a new one, came
into focus in the United Kingdom in January 1977, again as a

result of proposed legislation. As with personnel legislation it is incredible that legislation had to be resorted to in such an obvious matter as employee participation in the businesses which provide their livelihood. The causes go back a long way into industrial history, to workers' councils, co-operatives and joint consultative committees formed by individuals in companies, often following pressures from union officials.

On the management side briefing groups, advocated in the United Kingdom by the Industrial Society, brought some principles and system into the process of managers keeping their employees informed of what is happening and of problems and objectives. Individual line managers who have been so inclined have introduced their own methods of communication and participation into their departments. The open door style has grown and barriers to direct contact with line managers have been broken down significantly since the war. This, however, has affected the problem only to a limited extent. The splintered approach, that of participation with individuals on isolated occasions, is divisive and not to be recommended except in dealing with strictly personal matters.

The Committee of Enquiry on Industrial Democracy set about investigating this matter (under the chairmanship of Lord Bullock – a distinguished academic and writer on historical subjects), following an announcement of its formation in the House of Commons in August 1975. Almost two years elapsed before their report was presented and it is a thorough, highly interesting document. Since it was not implemented many of its worthwhile messages remain unheeded and will disappear but there is no doubt that it has been moderately successful in drawing attention to and stimulating thought about the subject. Line managers who did not read it at the time will find it almost a textbook on the subject and interesting to read even now, since if participation in a more organised and nationally suitable form had been introduced the state of communication over the past two difficult years would have ensured a clearer understanding of approaching survival problems by all employees. Although this has not yet been applied by legislation as a particular concept there are two areas of participation which are required and line managers should be aware of them. They are:

(a) *Proposed redundancies.* Consultative obligations are placed on employers and there are specific procedures for informing employee representatives and the Department of Employment about impending redundancy situations.

(b) *Health and safety at work.* The basic requirement is the preparation and implementation of a company health and safety policy plus the appointment of health and safety representatives. This is a big area of consultation and participation which, if successfully introduced, can pave the way for other forms of participation without legislation being imposed.

The Industry Act 1976 covers disclosure of information, and consequently participation in general terms on the basis of increased general knowledge, in annual reports, house journals and any other appropriate medium. Information about company organisation, its productivity, plans, prospects, industrial relations and state in the industry of which it forms a part are examples of communications matters which would be appropriate. Line managers should certainly get into the habit of reading their company's annual report as it is a highly informative document. A telephone call to the company secretary will produce a copy without any difficulty. The line manager's usual complaint that is it not understandable by the non-financial manager is valid but pressure from line management to have it explained could produce a briefing session, or short in-company seminar, conducted by the finanacial director. This is a very good opportunity for communication and participation at that level on a very worthwhile topic. Many annual reports now contain a non-technical supplement illustrating pictorially or graphically the position and performance of the business and projections into the future in an easily understood form.

BENEFITS OF PARTICIPATION

Some line managers will continue to feel that the introduction of participation will be time consuming and only marginally useful. They will feel that the majority of their employees will be content to get on with their work whilst the managers worry about running the business. This may be the right attitude for their particular situation but in circumstances where the need for, and usefulness of, participation are established the following benefits can be expected:

- Better understanding.
- More co-operation.
- Stronger motivation.
- Greater job satisfaction.
- Improved working relations.
- Better decision-making.
- Improved commitment by employees to decisions which they have helped to make.

To line managers who are continuously seeking development in these areas, the benefits of participation are obvious. At the moment they can be introduced as good management and not as a result of imposition by legislation. Line managers who take the initiative in matters of this kind will be in a position of positive leadership, which will be a refreshing state of affairs for many of them.

FUTURE OF LEGISLATION

It is now established that legislation, devised by a political party in government at a particular time, will influence the responsibilities of line management by its effect upon personnel management, participation and industrial relations. The next few years will see serious and continuing attempts by government not only to modify existing legislation in accordance with the pressures and priorities of the times, but to continue the reduction of discretionary areas and imposition of penalties where considered appropriate.

Attempts will grow to regulate and reduce union influence and authority in negative areas and to increase their impact in areas leading to greater productivity. The line manager's role will be to understand and apply this legislation to the day-to-day management of an operation, supported by communication, participation and implementation. An additional responsibility will be to ensure that subordinates in positions of authority are equally knowledgeable and are not creating problems through lack of information, training, guidance and support.

REFERENCES

United Kingdom legislation:

- Equal Pay Act 1970
- Health and Safety at Work Act 1974
- Trade Union and Labour Relations Act 1974
- Employment Protection Act 1975
- Industry Act 1975
- Sex Discrimination Act 1975
- Report of the Commission of Inquiry into Industrial Democracy 1977 (Bullock Report)
- Employment Protection (Consolidation) Act 1978
- Employment Act 1980.

11 The Right People in the Right Jobs: The Future

The previous chapters have shown that the question of people in business must not be left to chance in the future and that the company's prosperity, of which the prosperity of management is a part, must benefit from a greater attention by the line manager. It is now possible to generalise in two directions, the first of which is the relationship between organisational development and people development, the second the problem of growth after recession.

ORGANISATIONAL DEVELOPMENT AND ITS RELATIONSHIP WITH PERSONNEL DEVELOPMENT

This book has frequently referred to the vocabulary of management. One of its terms is 'organisation development', which means precisely what it says. As this book is primarily intended for managers who do not have access to a personnel manager operating in such areas as manpower planning, getting value from and fully utilising the company's total labour force, motivation and job satisfaction, very little reference has been made to the role of personnel management as a specialist function. This is deliberate as it is a subject which has received adequate treatment in the

141

literature of organisation and general management.

The treatment of personnel management as a function of line management, rather than as a special function, has been emphasised and it still applies, whether there is a personnel professional in the business or not. To develop organisations by developing people is a priority of personnel management today and it implies the need to be aware of this, and give it treatment appropriate to the whole organisation which involves much more than a line management responsibility. Whilst the line manager must see to it within his own department, the issue needs board attention.

Reference has been made from time to time, and especially in Chapter 8 which dealt with the promotion and development of people, to the fact that the organisation must facilitate development. All the matters discussed in this book are significant in organisational development.

(a) The utilisation and appreciation of value of people focuses on how this can be taken advantage of organisationally.

(b) Identifying and describing the jobs to be done will describe the total work load and suggest how it should be organised.

(c) Recruiting the right people by attention to interviewing techniques and selection methods implies better selection and requires better organisation to use the benefits of improved selection.

(d) Matching people to their jobs requires organisation which can be capable of greater efficiency because of the elimination of misfit people and misfit jobs.

(e) Introduction of people to the company, and the jobs they will be doing, will eliminate the bad start and require organisation capable of benefiting from this by making people effective more quickly.

(f) Promotion and development of people cannot happen without an organisation capable of allowing promotion and development, in fact requiring it to happen.

(g) Through appraisal and reward it is possible to know how people are performing and if they are producing the output necessary to generate rewards.

(h) Human and working relations based upon effective communication and participation designed to break down an 'us and them' atmosphere which strikes at the roots of the organisation.

Though organisation will differ from firm to firm within a given line of business, the above factors are common to all. The relationship between organisations and these factors needs to be investigated further; while a certain amount of research has been started there is much yet to be done. Line managers who can develop an appreciation of this relationship, not only themselves but in line management colleagues and directors, can regard themselves as being tuned in to a future priority in running their businesses. Like personnel management, organisational development is continuously changing in the light of both internal and external developments. This change of outlook is particularly important for the family firm, which is still more widespread than is popularly supposed, as the problems of both personnel and organisational development become acute in such firms in two circumstances:

1 When they begin to run out of management talent and interest in the family.
2 When they begin to run out of family.

In either situation there will be a need for new blood from outside and the family business which feels that it can engage from outside high-calibre people whose terms of reference include survival of the family business will be disappointed if they rely on personnel development only. There will have to be organisational development as well, because the new person will inevitably want to, and have to, organise and control affairs in a different way from the family. A special aspect of this particular change will be human and, especially, working relations.

GROWTH AFTER THE RECESSION

After a period of economic depression, as experienced throughout the industrialised world in the early 1980s, businesses which have survived will rise again and in addition new businesses will be created. The opportunities available to line managers in such a situation are both challenging and exciting. Antiquated attitudes will have no place in the equipment of those who are going to lead their businesses, and themselves, out of depression and into growth. Equally out of place will be an amateurish approach to the right people in the right jobs, and managers who do not work systematically through the stages advocated in this book will find they are quickly facing the problems of the past all over again. Progress in this area must be based upon the belief that the human resource has been continually underutilised and that profitable productivity is the key to this growth. The conversion of management attitudes from those appropriate to survival to those appropriate for growth is a major challenge to all levels from the owner or chairman to the unit supervisor. Survival attitudes have been successful in saving many businesses with their 'backs to the wall', which traditionally brings out the best in people. Line managers are often brilliant under these conditions. Progress will be based upon the following stages supported by adequate thinking processes and changes in company philosophy:

TAKING STOCK IS THE FIRST THING TO DO

As the worldwide recession eases, the time will come to strengthen slimmed-down business muscle. Before this can be done line managers must take stock of the human resource still available to them. In a slimming operation it is inevitable that people losses will occur in areas where they can least be spared, and that people sorely needed will leave of their own accord. Where there have been redundancies on the last in first out principle this state of affairs is very likely. To take stock the line manager will have to put into practice the content of Chapter 9 and organise a systematic appraisal. Groupings of age, temperament, qualifications and experience will emerge which will give a picture of the department. The use of personality tests, and in particular temperament tests, may be essential here in which case Chapter 5 will be helpful. There can be no progress along the path to knowing what is needed if line managers do not know what they already have and a sound appraisal will later prove the worth of the time and money spent on it. The analysis of existing inadequate resources before adding new will be an area of new activity to many line managers and they should know when to seek help. It should be sought and not left to another day.

STRENGTHENING THE EXISTING – BEFORE CONSIDERING THE NEW

There will be a trap here for the unprepared in confusion between strengthening the existing and adding the new. In the early stages growth can be discarded as a factor since to add growth on to an insecure foundation will build a structure destined to collapse. This strengthening of the foundation is clearly the next stage and relates to improving the state of current productivity, initially assuming no short-term growth. For many line managers a big problem will immediately appear. What is the productivity in the first place? So guidance will be needed about the relevant parameters of the organisation. This is a neglected training area since many managers do not know the parameters and would not be equipped to act on them if they did. Those managers who have been given the opportunity to attend external management courses will understand performance criteria, but in many cases, unfortunately, the chance to apply them in the department will not have occurred either because of lack of information and statistics or of time in which to make use of them. One of the high-priority training needs for line managers in relation to growth will be an appreciation of business and productivity figures indicating the true state of the activity being managed and the need to get them in time to take some positive action. The availability of information too late to be of value is a common complaint at line management level. In-company courses are advocated to remedy this situation and avoid moving forward in the dark. Chapter 6 deals with the matching of people to jobs on the assumption that there is adequate knowledge of the jobs – but this may be a false assumption. If it is, it must be realised there is no way round this matter – the knowledge has to be gathered and the line manager is the person to get it. As a direct result of this analysis, whether growth is being contemplated or not and whether performance criteria are available or not, some obvious facts will stare the manager in the face. These are:

(a) Allocation of numbers of employees to different groups of task with the observation that there are still too many in some and not enough in others.

(b) Age brackets indicating bunching in certain groups and probably revealing missing young people because of recession recruiting restrictions. Job opportunity schemes in the United Kingdom may be a short-term remedy for this.

(c) Grouping of employees over sixty, indicating a normal or early retirement need and immediate plans for training of younger people to succeed them.

(d) Strong performers capable of pulling more load immediately and who are seeking an opportunity to do so.

(e) Weak performers who could improve quickly by a short training programme.

(f) Very weak performers who have survived for some reason and who should be moved out of their jobs as a matter of some urgency.

(g) Problem employees who are causing friction, conflict and sowing seeds of discontent. There may be truth in their complaints which could point the way to rapid short-term improvement: on the other hand, there may not be.

All these points must have attention under the heading of strengthening the existing and as confidence grows there will be a stimulation to look in new directions related to growth.

TACKLING GROWTH – TOO COMPLICATED FOR THE LINE MANAGER

It is usually accepted that the departmental line manager is not going to set the pace directly after recession. One of top management's biggest tasks will be to change the acceptance

of this as a fact and make it quite clear to all in the company
(participation) that everybody has a contribution to make.
Old-fashioned company suggestion schemes were always
evidence of this and if the right spirit is generated there could
be a flow of ideas. This is not to suggest that businesses will
pull out of recession on the back of glorified suggestion
schemes. It is to suggest that this is an opportunity to revive
morale, interest and caring about the business in a battered
labour force – especially its line managers, who are suffering
from acute depression and exhaustion following the struggle
to survive. The owners and directors of companies will have
growth permanently on their board agendas and line
managers should be looking to them to show:

- The board is growth minded.
- It is making a critical appraisal of the existing business,
  what it is there to do and what will its markets be.
- If it was a United Kingdom business in the past, it has
  positive intentions to get into overseas markets in the
  future.
- It is arranging market research followed by identification
  of the resources it will need, especially overseas.
- It is aware of government incentive schemes and financial
  aid available to it.
- It is making a technical overhaul of its products or services
  to assess their relevance in the 1980s and if they have little
  relevance what diversification possibilities exist.
- Who among them is the prime mover for growth and do
  line managers have confidence in the person appointed
  by the board?
- What opportunities are available for ideas to flow upwards
  and what is the correct procedure for making them flow?
- What use is being made of external organisations, such as
  consultants, to bring fresh air and an informed, unbiased
  contribution to the proceedings?

Line managers who feel that these matters are insufficiently
appreciated by their superiors should seek every opportunity
to be of service to their businesses, and themselves, by
raising the subjects either formally or informally.

CONSOLIDATION

Following the identification of a growth path, and decision about the strengthening process to be applied, line managers can now begin to apply Chapters 2 to 9 in full taking account of legislation, communication and participation in Chapter 10.

A vital aspect of this process is the relationship between management and unions. In the United Kingdom there is evidence that the pressures of recession have removed some of the militancy which had crept into industrial relations. There is, in addition, much evidence to show that union members have minds of their own, can weigh up a situation for themselves and are no longer prepared to 'toe the line' drawn by their shop stewards and union officials.

Although the United Kingdom Industrial Relations Act 1971 was superseded by new legislation in 1975, one of the good things about it was its supporting code of practice. The following quotation from it sets the scene for better communication in future, if it is adhered to:

'Good industrial relations need to be developed with the framework of an efficient organisation.'

'Managers at the highest level should give, and show that they give, just as much attention to industrial relations as to such functions as finance, marketing, production or administration.'

'... the primary responsibility for their promotion (good industrial relations) rests with management. It should, therefore, take the initiative in creating and developing them.'

'All managers should receive training in the industrial relations implications of their jobs. This is as necessary for line managers, including supervisors, as for personnel managers.'

'Management should recognise that each employee has individual needs and aspirations at work and should take this into account in its day-to-day conduct of business. In particular, management should recognise the employee's need to achieve a sense of satisfaction in the job and should provide for it so far as practicable.'

This code has now been absorbed into the work of the Arbitration, Conciliation and Advisory Service (ACAS) and is publicised by it extensively. Line managers should not only be concerned about the selection, motivation and performance of their employees in isolation but in similar matters applicable to the shop stewards who represent these workers. Participation (see Chapter 10) must increase and line managers should be prime movers in ensuring that it does so, constructively, in the departments for which they have responsibilities.

MANPOWER PLANNING

This may be impossible because of external unknowns and unforseen developments. It is a local and national problem. So far corporate planning stimulated by politicians, economists and academics has a slim history but growth will strengthen its contribution. Unfortunately, at the moment negative prediction of the figures for unemployment in the United Kingdom has become a continuing topic for political speeches and the media, and is contributing greatly to the gloomy atmosphere. Assessments of such matters as:

- where the business is going
- what will be its products
- what will be its markets
- what resources will it have

will have to be made by the people at the top of the business but line managers who can contribute should be prepared to put their ideas forward. It is only on the basis of the best judgement available at the time that manpower planning will be a possibility. Line managers will then be faced with an obligation to fill employment at their own level and each individual manager who can plan to take at least one person out of unemployment will be doing the right thing, but only if it is the right person in the right job. To bring in young people who have been demotivated by unemployment and train them will strengthen the business. To blend this new talent with the old, combining enthusiasm with experience, is an exciting manpower planning challenge.

CONCLUSIONS

In surveying the personnel situation it has been possible to identify the future role of the line manager with it. If the ingredients of management are

- technical knowledge
- administrative ability
- skill at getting and keeping the right people

then it is further possible to envisage much of the first two being delegated but none of the third. People are the foundation of any business activity, as they are the life in it and operators of the technical and administrative aspects of it. The traditional path to management is by competence in the work of the department. This does not always mean competence with people, and it is unfortunate that many potentially good managers cannot realise their full potential because they do not have this competence and have been given no opportunity to acquire it. The research work of behavioural scientists and industrial sociologists is illuminating attitudes and desires of people in relation to their working lives and the managers of the future will have interesting opportunities to put some of these findings into practice. The introduction of organizational development, highlighting its dependence upon people development, into the principles of management will bring people-minded managers into more contact with organisation and control.

Personnel legislation with its attendant Codes of Practice has formalised many desirable and high-priority personnel matters which, when added together, mean better personnel management as well as better industrial relations. Cultivation of the team spirit, provision of more interesting jobs and the opportunity to develop and be rewarded against performance must bring the best out of people and revive some of the caring about the long-term prosperity of society, which means all of us, instead of the short-term prosperity of the individual.

The future is in the hands of the line manager. The ones who survive to best advantage will be those who have worked out their own methods, in their own situations, of getting the best out of their own people by getting the right people in the right jobs. If this book can contribute to that it will have served its purpose.

Index

153